Sun, Sea and Super Yachts

The essential beginner's guide to a career in yachting

The Career Concierge

For all our new seafarers...

Table of Contents

Sun, Sea and Super Yachts	1
Message from Clare	7
Sarah's Seafarer Story	9
CHAPTER ONE	11
What actually is a yacht?	11
Alice's Seafarer Story	21
Chapter Two	23
What are the downsides of working on board?	23
Ian's Seafarer Story	31
Chapter Three	33
The Practicalities Of Yachting Life	33
YACHT LAYOUT	37
Cara's Seafarer Story	41
Chapter Four	43
Which yachting role is right for you?	43
Mia's Seafarer Story	73
Chapter Five	75
What to expect from your yachting contract	75
Joel's Seafarer Story	85
Chapter Six	87
Training and qualifications	87
Michael's Seafarer Story	113
Chapter Seven	115
What to do before you travel	115

Olivia's Seafarer Story	127
Chapter Eight	129
The Job Hunt	129
Alfie's Seafarer Story	157
Chapter Nine	159
Interview tips and techniques	159
Harry's Seafarer Story	177
Mary's Seafarer Story	179
Glossary	181
Thank you	186
Resources	188
Copyright and Disclaimer	189

Message from Clare

So... you're thinking about a career in yachting?

You've picked up the right book! I've been a part of the yachting industry since 2008 and have experienced the highs and lows of a working life on the water. I also know how the industry works on dry land. Most of my personal yachting career has been spent on the recruitment side, and I've guided many hundreds of people just like you into seafaring jobs.

I sat down to write this book in response to the many questions I receive on a daily basis from yachting hopefuls. This book is designed to be a complete guide for starting out in the industry.

In it, I'll advise you on every step of establishing yourself in your new career, from what training you'll need to where to go to get work and what to expect once you've found it.

Read on to learn:
- The types of positions that are offered
- The qualifications you'll need
- How to find work
- What to pack
- Successful interview techniques
- What happens on board a yacht
- The different types of yachts you'll need to know about

- Why super yachts might not be exactly what you expect
- The realities of life living on board
- Salary guidelines
- Real life stories from crew past and present

So if all of this sounds appealing to you, let's get on board and get going!

Many new crew members begin their career by heading straight to a yachting hub with their bags packed, ready to sail. I've spoken to a lot of hopefuls who have assumed they would be able to walk straight into a job. A very small percentage of lucky ones do. Unfortunately, that is not the truth of the industry today. It can actually be very difficult to secure your first position, so you need to do what you can to stand out from the crowd.

There is good news here. Being proactive by doing your research and getting educated about the industry is likely to earn you the respect of potential employers and crew agents alike!

I'd like to take this opportunity to congratulate you on making the brave decision to try something new and embark on a career that's both exciting and rewarding.

Best of luck!

Clare

Throughout this book, you'll find real-life stories from yachting crew members. My hope is that these stories will both inspire you and help you to prepare for the challenges ahead.

Sarah's Seafarer Story

Sarah spent five years as a stewardess on a super yacht after a successful career as a Dive Instructor. She's now 34 and is trying out life on land!

I began thinking seriously about working in the super yacht industry in my mid-twenties while working as a Dive Instructor. A friend showed me an advert in a charter magazine for a yacht that travelled extensively, mainly to the top dive destinations in the world. It sounded like the perfect lifestyle.

Eight months later I was lucky enough to spot a recruitment call from the same boat! I already had the qualifications I needed, so I took a deep breath and got in touch.

The Captain called for a telephone interview and asked how soon I could meet the boat. Being a complete newbie, I suggested two weeks... I was told that if I wanted the job I had to be there in three days! This was much quicker than I'd expected, but I knew it was unlikely I'd get such a good opportunity again. I booked a flight for the next day.

I packed, said goodbye to my family, and left home in such a hurry that it wasn't until the second leg of my flight that I began to feel nervous. I arrived at the airport feeling jet-lagged and sleep deprived, but I tried not to show it. The Chief Stewardess and 2nd Stewardess were waiting for me in Arrivals. There was so much to do that I almost forgot my nerves!

We arrived at the dock, and I got my first glimpse of the 38-metre motor yacht. It was older than I'd expected, but it hardly mattered when it was docked in such a gorgeous tropical location. The 2nd Stewardess showed me to the cabin we'd be sharing. I realised why I was told to travel light; it was very compact! My new uniform was waiting for me, and I put it on right away.

The working day on the yacht started at 7.30am. Everyone had a job to do, and even on my first day, I was expected to jump straight in. It was a huge learning curve, but the crew were fantastic. I really appreciated their support, especially as I adjusted to life on board. It was a much more controlled environment than I was used to; there were safety rules and regulations to follow as well as the reality of living and working with the same group of people 24/7.

There were moments when I questioned whether the yachting industry was right for me. But for every one of these moments, there were incredible experiences and opportunities that I would never have had if I hadn't been brave enough to book that first flight!

Chapter One

What actually is a yacht?

When you think of a yacht, what springs to mind?

You may be picturing a high-end luxury ship or alternatively a sailing vessel built for racing. Though these images are very different, neither of them are wrong.

The word *yacht* comes from the Dutch word *jacht*, which means 'hunt'. Originally Dutch *jachts* were fast ships built to hunt down pirates!

In modern-day terms, a yacht is a boat or ship used for pleasure cruising or racing. They can be powered by either a sail or an engine and can vary hugely in size.

A general yacht size guide includes Super Yachts, Mega Yachts and Giga Yachts, but despite my best efforts to research the size definitions I could not find any accurate data on the breakdown, so my version is as follows.

- A **super yacht** is a vessel over 24m in length
- A **mega yacht** is a vessel over 50m in length
- A **giga yacht** is a vessel over 100m in length

As for what comes next, who knows? Yachts are just getting bigger and bigger these days!

Who owns these yachts?

For many people, owning a motor yacht is seen as the ultimate in luxury living. Standards on board are notoriously high, and many vessels endeavour to offer a seven-star service to the high net-worth individuals who own them.

This kind of vessel costs a fortune to run, so even most celebrities can't afford to own one themselves. This isn't to say they don't participate in the onboard lifestyle. Many actors, sports personalities, and musicians regularly charter yachts or get invited on as guests, but even their salaries don't usually stretch far enough to buy one. So if you're thinking about working on a yacht because you want to work for movie stars, you may be disappointed!

Most yachts on the sea are owned by billionaire and multi-millionaire businessmen and women.

Who builds yachts?

There are numerous high-end boat-building companies working in locations scattered around the world. Just some of the bigger names you are likely to become familiar with are:
- Feadship
- Oceanfast
- Benetti
- Azimut

- Amels
- Heesen
- Perini Navi
- Sunseeker
- Princess
- Palmer Johnson
- Lurssen
- Amels

How many yachts are there worldwide?

It's difficult to give an exact number for this, but it's been calculated that at present there are around five thousand yachts dotted around the globe. The vast majority of these bounce between the Mediterranean, the US, and the Caribbean, but in recent years, more yachts are frequently leaving the 'milk run' and travelling to other destinations around the globe.

How many yachts are being built annually?

Again, this data isn't easy to come by, but the general expectation in the industry is that there are approximately two hundred yachts in production on a yearly basis.

How much do they cost to buy?

Are you sitting down? Absolutely millions, which is why even some big name celebrities cannot afford to own one, and after the build costs, there is the interior decoration to consider, all before hiring the crew. Also keeping in mind that to charter a yacht can cost a pretty penny too. An example is an 80m yacht costing around $1 million to rent for the week on top of which the client has to pay for food, drinks, fuel, berthing fees, crew tips.

How much do they cost to run?

There are a lot of running costs involved in keeping a yacht on the water. These costs typically amount to around 10-15% of the overall purchase price every year. Running costs include factors such as; crew salaries, berthing fees, fuel, crew food, and ongoing maintenance.

Is there much difference between working on a yacht and a cruise ship?

There is sometimes a little confusion about the difference between working on a yacht and other large water vessels such as cruise ships. Even though modern yachts are getting bigger and bigger (and indeed are sometimes referred to as mini cruise ships), yachts are still generally smaller and run very differently than their cruising counterparts.

The best way to think of a cruise ship is as a small floating town. They have shopping malls, a variety of restaurants, swimming pools, bars and entertainment venues and can accommodate thousands of guests on each trip.

Many cruise ships can have high standards when it comes to customer service, but even these are nothing in comparison to the level of service and personal touches that are found on a super yacht.

If a cruise ship is a small floating town, a yacht is like an exclusive boutique hotel or perhaps a private palace. Most accommodate approximately twelve guests, though they do take on much larger groups of people for parties. As you can imagine, the level of personal service a team of staff are able to provide to a couple of people is very different to what is offered on a full-capacity cruise ship.

Service expectations aren't all that's different. The average salary for cruise ship staff is a lot lower than yachting staff. There is a rationale to this. As a cruise ship employee, you would have structured hours of work and downtime along with a set role. As a yacht employee, this would be unlikely to be the case. Because yachts have much fewer staff, employees are often expected to keep going until all the necessary work is done. This can involve long hours, late nights, night shifts, and split shifts, as well as being expected to help out in different departments when required.

Finally, working on a yacht is different to working on a cruise ship because of where you are likely to travel. Yachts are much smaller vessels, which means they're able to navigate their way to more remote, off-the-beaten-track places than a cruise ship. As yachts are usually privately owned, they're also more likely to travel to a variety of destinations rather than sticking to one or two set routes.

Motor yachts versus sailing yachts. What's the deal here?

Not all yachts are the same! The two categories are luxury motor yachts and sailing yachts. Both motor and sailing yachts can vary from small, classic or large and luxurious. However, most people find that life on a sailing yacht is a little more relaxed than on a motor yacht. This is because the owners are usually passionate sailors who look for crew who share that passion.

The hiring authorities involved will be looking for crew who come from a sailing background or have a keen interest in the world of sailing and are eager to learn more.

On a sailing yacht, it's normal for crew in all departments to be hands on with the sailing of the vessel. There's usually a strong ethos of all being in it together, so you'll be expected to help out in all areas. The salaries on a sailing yacht are generally a little lower to that of a motor yacht, but if that is a major concern for you, a sailing yacht career probably isn't right for you. Joining the crew of a sailing yacht is about far more than just a job. It's about the experience and the lifestyle.

Motor yachts typically have a very different culture to their classic sailing counterparts. They tend to be more regimented in terms of how they are run, and they offer more generous salaries and benefits packages. A job on a motor yacht would be less ideal for people who are passionate about sailing as you would be unlikely to have much to do with the cruising of the vessel. Instead, motor yacht crew are employed to provide a high level of service to guests and to clean and maintain the boat.

Should you choose to work on a small or large vessel?

The size of a yacht can have a big impact on what it's like to live and work onboard. I wouldn't advise anyone to rule out work on board a smaller yacht.

Smaller vessels can be fantastic places to work for a number of reasons. Yes, the owners will still expect a high level of service, *but* these boats can often be far more family-oriented. Teamwork will be vitally important, as you'll need to assist in areas outside of your job description. This could mean that deckhands may need to help the stewardesses with service or that stewardesses may need to help on deck with wash downs and mooring procedures. In some cases, smaller yachts offer combined roles onboard such as Deck/Engineer. If you're prepared to really get involved, this can be hugely beneficial experience-wise as you'll have the opportunity to get a good all-round view and experience of the requirements of each department.

On larger vessels, the general rule is that you normally only work in your own department. Of course, life on any kind of yacht can be unpredictable, and you may sometimes be called upon to get your hands dirty in a different department. However, on a day-to-day basis, you can expect to work in your set role with very specific duties outlined. Crew on larger vessels sometimes enjoy more structured work hours and rest as they have enough team members in each department to offer a shift pattern.

What do you need to know about private yachts versus charter yachts?

Let's start with private vessels. These yachts are used by the owner, their families, and any guests they choose to invite on board. Some private boat owners even live on board full time.

A private boat can be incredibly busy if the owner uses the boat a lot. Between cruising and visiting various destinations, you may find that it's as 'full on' as working on a charter vessel. However, you will find many private vessels are used by the owners just for holidays and business trips. In these cases, they can be far less demanding workplaces simply because crew are likely to have more downtime between periods of owner use. Though work is likely to be extremely busy when the owner is on board (and you will be subject to all the same service expectations as any other yacht), when the owners aren't on board, you may find you work more regular hours, perhaps even something along the lines of 8am-5pm.

Things are a little different on a charter boat. Guests will pay an eye-wateringly large fee to hire the boat for a week or two. They'll also pay for whatever food and drinks they require as well as fuel and berthing costs. It's normal, but not obligatory, for guests to tip the crew if they feel they've had an enjoyable stay.

Life on board a charter boat can be very busy and demanding, as crew will need to accommodate guests as much as possible. Let's put it this way; if a charter guest wants to stay up and party until 4 am... you'll be staying up too to make sure drinks are refilled and snacks are provided. Of course, some of the other guests on board may have gone to bed early and will be up at 7 am for breakfast as usual. You should work in shifts for this, but it can still be very disruptive in regards to sleep patterns.

Though lots of charter guests will tip generously, you're likely to work very hard for your money during these trips. And that's not all. On a popular charter boat, you can say goodbye to one set of guests, and then only have twenty-four or forty-eight hours to turn the boat around, re-provision, and catch your breath before you welcome the next group on board.

Alice's Seafarer Story

Alice started work as a Yacht Stewardess at the age of eighteen. Six years later, she is still hard at work in the industry and loving it. Here is a day-in-the-life story of her time as a 2nd Stewardess on a 50m Yacht.

My most recent position was as 2nd Stewardess on a 50m Yacht. This role was a little different to standard crew work as we spent five months docked in the Amels shipyard in Holland undergoing a significant re-fit. Please don't assume this was a relaxed position. We were busy from dawn till dusk!

During the re-fit, we lived on land at an apartment near to the shipyard. The work was done over the winter season, which meant we were down to two stewardesses, and the chef was away on annual leave.

Each morning, we began work by dropping the crew off at the boat and then rushing to the local supermarket. There we stocked up for the makeshift crew mess we had set up in the shipyard and got enough provisions for the day's lunch and dinner, plus basics for the fridges in all three crew apartments.

Once the shopping was done and put away, we were able to get started on the real morning's work: cleaning and laundry. This involved cleaning all three apartments to the same standards that would be expected on board and turning over the laundry for all the crew. The laundry was a bit of a nightmare as we had gone from using an amazing industrial machine on board to standard household washer and dryer.

My fellow stewardess would prepare lunch for the whole team, which included the two of us, ten crew members, and four daily workers. We'd then take it back down to the shipyard, warm it up in the crew mess, and serve it up for a line of very hungry workers! At this point, we'd have a short break to eat something ourselves and catch up with what had been happening at the shipyard. Talk usually turned to the crew's evening plans, which almost always involved the gym. There wasn't much else to do in the area.

After lunch, we'd stay at the shipyard in order to meet with the project manager. Together we'd discuss the progress that was being made in the interior of the ship and any projects that were near completion.

Once the meeting was done, we'd spend the rest of the afternoon on board. This time was used to check the workmanship to ensure everything was up to standard and to keep on top of onboard cleaning.

Somewhere between 5-6pm, we'd bundle the whole crew back into the van and head back to the apartments. The evening would be spent at the gym or relaxing before sitting down as a group for dinner.

...And then we'd do it all again the following day.

Chapter Two

What are the downsides of working on board?

Before you make a final decision to join the yachting industry, you'll want to make sure that you have a good understanding of what it's *really* like to work on board.

In this chapter, I've set out some of the factors about the industry that are often considered the downsides. If you think one or more of these might be a deal breaker, be honest! It is better to be realistic about what you want from a job!

If the factors below don't faze you, you're likely to find that a yachting career could be a really great fit.

Owner expectations will be extremely high

Yacht owners and onboard guests will always expect a very high level of service. All the work you do while on board will need to be absolutely perfect. Professionalism and discretion are also seriously important.

Owners and guests will expect their crew to take care of their every need from the moment they wake up in the morning until when they retire in the evening (or early hours). Crew members will also be expected to be well groomed and display a certain level of decorum whatever the situation at hand.

Remember, the people who own or charter these yachts are paying hundreds of thousands of dollars or pounds for the privilege. They therefore obviously expect the very best. It will be your job to ensure that they receive the level of service they expect and that they have the most enjoyable experience while on board.

You'll need to work harder than you ever have in your life

Many new workers in the yachting industry are surprised at just how different the lifestyle is to anything they've experienced before. Let me reiterate; this really is a job like no other!

Anyone who thinks there is easy money to be made will have a very big shock. This is a job in which you are providing high-level service to the super rich. It's certainly not easy (being good at service is an art form in itself), and not everyone can pull it off.

When you're on duty you must always be polite, well presented, and have a smile on your face. This is the case even if you've only had four hours sleep, your feet are killing you, and you're suffering from seasickness. When you work on a yacht, there's no calling in sick. You just have to get on with it and create the illusion that all is well. You'll need to adapt to the mindset that the guest is the most important person and how tired or poorly you are feeling really doesn't matter.

It can be difficult to adapt to living in your workplace

One of the reasons that yachting is so different from other types of jobs is that you can't go home at the end of your shift. When you accept a crew position, you are signing up to a lifestyle in which you will live, eat, sleep and breathe yachting, 24 hours a day, 7 days a week. The yacht will become your home. You will have breakfast, lunch and dinner with your work colleagues. The only 'private space' you'll have will most likely be your bed space in a shared cabin.

This isn't to say that you'll get on with all of your colleagues all the time. You probably won't. But if you do feel there's a personality clash, it's best to keep it to yourself and get on with it. After all, you have to live with these people! Though you will come across them occasionally, in yachting, there really is no room for big egos.

Days off are likely to be a rare luxury

When the season is in full swing, you'll need to accept that you're highly unlikely to get any days off, and yes, that includes weekends. It's normal for crew members to work for several weeks and sometimes months with back-to-back guest trips without a break.

You can, of course, book holiday time, but it's likely to be refused if you request a vacation during the busy season. Plans can change at the last minute. You may find that the weekend you've booked to attend a wedding is now when the boss is coming to use his boat, and your time off is cancelled. You will need to be prepared to miss important birthdays, family Christmases, weddings, and other important occasions. I know one crew member who went eight years without spending Christmas with their family. Another has had to turn down every wedding invitation for a decade. This can be really hard on you emotionally, so you need to be prepared.

Staying in contact with the outside world can be a logistical nightmare

How addicted are you to your smartphone? This is an important question as keeping in touch with friends and family can be difficult due to the time difference, location, signal, roaming charges, and calling credit.

Yachts of today generally have Internet access. However, you may not have unlimited access to it. Some yachts reduce the time crew can use the Internet, as guests must take priority, especially if the connection is slow.

As for socialising with friends, spending time shopping, or even going to the gym, you'll need to accept that these are not always possible. Your boat is likely to be actively cruising, on anchor, or docked in a shipyard that could be far away from town.

Your days will be spent following orders

Before you even step foot on a yacht, *please* consider whether you have the right personality type for it. Most importantly, you need to decide whether you're the kind of person who can take orders from your peers without questioning their motives. This is important, as taking and following orders will be the mainstay of your day. Yes, you'll need to be resilient, breathe deep, and perform your daily duties with enthusiasm.

If you find this aspect of the job tricky, it can sometimes help to remember there's normally a reason for it. Orders are given and rules are put in place for two main reasons; to give paying guests or owners the experience and service that they expect, and most importantly, to keep everyone on board safe.

To be honest, the road to success in this line of work is quite simple; keep a positive attitude at all times, and you will go far!

Seasickness can be a serious problem

Trust me when I say that seasickness is no laughing matter. If you've experienced seasickness in the past, you will need to think very carefully about whether you are going to be physically suited to a yachting career. Some crew members who are initially unwell do adapt and get over their seasickness... but others do not.

When I started out in recruitment, my predecessor told me about an amazing stewardess he had put on a boat. Her work was very impressive, and the captain was thrilled, but they'd spent the first six months of her contract in port. As soon as they took the boat out, she became very sick indeed and quickly realised that her yachting career was over. Please learn from this experience, and make sure you've had at least some experience on a boat before you apply for a yachting crew role!

Privacy on board can be very hard to come by

The lack of privacy on a yacht can be tricky to adjust to. The space in which you'll be living will be very small, and your only personal space will be your bunk and the shelf next to it. Because of this, it's really important to respect the privacy of your fellow crew members. If you do, hopefully, they will pay you the same courtesy in return.

The longer you live and work on a yacht, the better you will become at reading your colleagues and understanding when they want to be left alone. In the meantime, I'd suggest you always follow the three basic rules below:

1. Respect closed curtains! Some yachts have curtains on the bunks in each cabin. If these curtains are closed, it probably means your cabin mate wants some alone time, peace, or sleep.

2. Don't use things that aren't yours without asking, even if they are in your cabin.

3. If your cabin mate is in bed by the time you retire, try to be respectful and quiet. They will have done a hard day's work just like you and sleep is precious!

Sharing a small cabin with a stranger is definitely a learning curve, but it will get much easier over time. I can also guarantee that there is no better way to really get to know someone! If you can be patient with each other and respect each other's privacy, you will no doubt become lifelong friends.

Ian's Seafarer Story

Ian is an American crew member, aged 30. He came to the Yachting industry after a career in the US Air Force. He's now spent five years in the industry and is still going! During his time on the water, he has worked as a Mate, a Super Yacht Security Officer, a Deckhand, and an Engineer.

My yachting career path has not been straightforward! I found my first job after moving to St Thomas USVI. It took a lot of work to get a position. I started by dock walking and then accepted my first gig without pay. This worked as I was prepared to just show up and say 'here I am, this is what can I do, I want to be part of this.' Eventually, I was made a mate of one of a fleet of five Farr 40 racing sailboats.

After this, I joined a 100m+ boat as a Security Officer. I then became a Deckhand before realising that I wanted to get into Engineering. This isn't always an easy route as you need qualifications to get a job and you need sea miles to get qualified! I avoided this by taking on the combined role of Deck/Engineer and building up enough credibility to become a 3rd Engineer. I'm now aiming to work my way through the ranks.

When I first joined the industry, people treated me pretty badly. They considered me a nobody who knew nothing, even though after my time in the Air Force and two tours in Afghanistan, I felt I had more life experience than most of the crew I had encountered. With much self-sacrifice and hard work, I was able to prove myself and became well known for my ethics. This reputation really helped when it came to putting myself forward for new positions.

One of my funny memories during my time in the industry happened while on a boat in the Philippines. We'd all bought mopeds to use while we were docked in a shipyard, but the 2nd Chef crashed his and damaged the paintwork. Without him knowing, the rest of us all pitched in and paid to have a local man give it a new paint job... in a vibrant fluorescent pink!

When he saw it, he threw his hands up, then fell to his knees with tears of laughter. The best part was that he rocked the hot pink moped all over town for the rest of our time in the yard. When the boat left, the local Filipino girls were desperate to get their hands on his moped!

Chapter Three
The Practicalities Of Yachting Life

Think you can handle the downsides? Great. Let's move on to the practicalities of working on a yacht. In this chapter, I've addressed what you'll find on a typical yacht, how they're laid out, and some of the duties you'll be expected to perform.

What can you expect to find on a yacht?

All yachts are different, and it's impossible to say exactly what you'll find onboard the boat you will end up working on. You may be surprised at how much can fit on board! Some bigger boats will have gyms, complete spa areas, entertainment rooms, and bar areas both inside and out!

Here are some of the areas generally found on board that you should get acquainted with:

Salon

The salon is the lounge area for use by the owners of the yacht and their guests. It often includes a bar and ample space for parties.

Master Cabin

The Master Cabin is the name given to the main bedroom on board. It's reserved for the owners or very special charter guests and is normally bigger and more luxurious than the guest cabins.

Guest Cabins

The bigger the yacht, (usually) the more guest cabins it'll have. Once again, these will be luxurious and well-equipped.

Bridge

The area of the ship where the boat is commanded

Day Head

This is the name given to the guest toilet on the main deck.

Pantry

On a boat, the pantry refers to the area the interior team use to make drinks, decorate cocktails, garnish plates, and organise linens whilst serving guests.

Galley

The galley, known to us land-based folk as the kitchen area, is where the chef and his team prepare their culinary delights!

Crew Quarters

This is where you'll find the crew cabins. They're normally situated below the main deck and will all be shared rooms unless you're the captain or the chief engineer, in which case you *may* get your own cabin. Each cabin will have two to three single bunk beds along with shared wardrobe space and one shelf per person. The good news is that most cabins on newer built vessels have en-suite bathroom facilities.

Crew Mess

Crew break areas are referred to as the mess. Facilities will vary wildly from yacht to yacht. Some can be cramped and uncomfortable, but others can be generous with space. (Remember, it's all relative!)

The mess is where the crew eat, watch TV, and socialise. You can usually expect it to have fridges and cupboards well-stocked with food, so do watch your waistline!

How are yachts laid out?

Like I have said it will vary but take a look at the illustration to see an example.

Some of the key yachting terms you will want to familiarise yourself with include: bow, stern, port side, starboard side, aft deck, middle deck, upper/sun deck, passarelle, bridge, fore peak...

These are all everyday terms on board, and it will speed things up considerably if you are already comfortable with using them before you start.

Yacht Layout

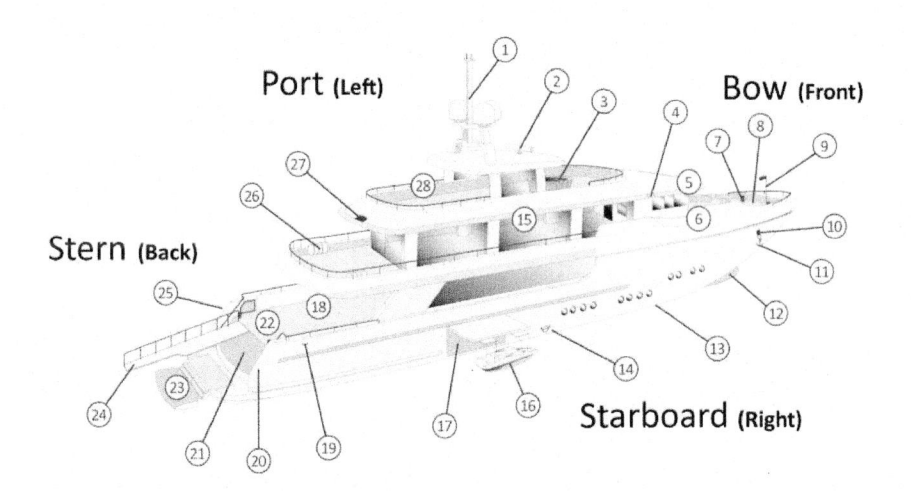

1. Mast
2. Radar
3. Jacuzzi
4. Navigation lights
5. Bridge
6. Starboard bridge wing
7. Capstans
8. Fore peak
9. Fore mast
10. Anchor pocket
11. Anchor
12. Bolbus bow
13. Water line
14. Load line
15. Bridge deck/Owners deck
16. Tender
17. Tender garage
18. Aft
19. Mooring fare leads
20. Starboard aft quarter
21. Lazarette
22. Main deck
23. Swim platform
24. Passarelle
25. Port aft quarter
26. Life rafts
27. Navigation lights
28. Sun deck/Top deck

What additional duties will you be responsible for?

Every crew member on board will have plenty of responsibilities relating to their primary role, be it stewardess, engineer, deckhand, or chef. However, there are a few additional duties that all crew members will be expected to take on.

Watch Duty

Every crew member will have to perform watch duty while working on board. This is normally done on a rota schedule and includes weekends. The rota will often change when the yacht is in 'guest mode'.

Watch duty is a twenty-four hour period, often running from 7.30am or 8am, depending on the rules set in place on that vessel.

When you're on watch duty you will be expected to perform duties including:
- Locking and unlocking exterior doors
- Raising the flag in the morning and taking it down at sunset
- Raising or lowering of the passarelle
- Turning on interior lights in the morning and turning them off in the evening
- Carrying out a complete walk around of the boat every few hours, checking for problems in the engine room, out on the deck and in the interior
- Checking the lines

- Answering the phone
- Carrying a pager to be notified of any alarms going off at any point, night or day

During watch duty you are not normally permitted to leave the vessel.

Captains and chief engineers don't normally do watch duty, but engineers usually have their own on-call rota. An engineer on call will need to be close to the vessel in case any alarms go off that they need to tend to.

Cleaning

Each crew member is responsible for the cleanliness and tidiness of their cabin. Depending on the yacht, you could even be subject to cabin inspections. Beware as there are sometimes penalties for the worst cabin after an inspection... double weekend watch anyone? Ouch!

It's also worth noting that while the stewardesses tend to be responsible for daily cleaning of the crew mess areas, it is still each crew member's responsibility to help clean up after meal times and assist with keeping the area tidy.

Cara's Seafarer Story

Cara is English and worked in the yachting industry as a stewardess for two years between 2009 and 2011. Here is her 'day in the life' of a typical day on a charter boat with twelve guests on board.

0600hrs: Chef is already in kitchen prepping. I arrive, turn on the coffee machine, lay the breakfast table, and tidy the salon, ready for the first guests. If there's time, I might grab a bowl of cereal and a coffee for myself.

0700hrs onwards: Guests begin to appear for smoothies, coffees, teas, and their breakfast. Each guest arrives in their own time so I usually continue to manage breakfast service until 1000. In quieter moments, I find out whether guests will be eating lunch on or off the boat, chill wine for later in the day, and make a shopping list for Chef in case there's time to get off the boat.

1000-1200hrs: Most guests (hopefully all of them!) depart the boat to explore the area. This is our time to do the cabins. This includes cleaning, remaking beds, changing towels, vacuuming, and dusting.

1200noon: Crew lunchtime. Usually, chef makes something simple but filling like pasta, meat, salad, and bread.

1230hrs: Preparations for guest lunch begins.

1300hrs: Lunch on deck, usually including a long affair of food and drinks service, followed by tidying up, of course.

1430 – 1800hrs: The afternoon involves a lot of multitasking! I offer drinks and snacks to guests, while also finding out about dinner plans, preparing wines for the evening, working in the laundry, carrying out cabin and bathroom checks, and doing any necessary cleaning.

1800hrs: Dinner preparations begin. I iron table linen, dress the tables, and lay up for dinner. I also change into my evening service uniform. If I'm really lucky, there might be time for a quick shower.

1830hrs: Time for guest aperitifs: cocktails in the bar and food from the chef.

1830 – 2200hrs: Full dinner service including a three-course meal, drinks, wine, snacks, and more drinks!

2200hrs: The washing up begins. This is a big task, as most dinner wear cannot go in the dishwasher. The exterior crew assists with this while we return to the laundry.

2300 – 0200hrs: Guests continue to enjoy their evening. I'm on call for drinks and service while doing the laundry.

0200hrs: The guests are hungry but the chef has finished for the night. I make cheese and ham toasties.

0300hrs: The guests finally retire to bed. I clean a final lot of glasses, put them away, and tidy up the deck and the salon.

0330hrs: I fall into bed, very tired.

Chapter Four

Which yachting role is right for you?

Once upon a time in the yachting industry, you could easily land your first job through dock walking or word of mouth, phone number on the back of a cigarette packet, have no formal qualifications, and still do pretty well.

This is no longer the case. As the industry has grown, it has become more regulated. Before you even start searching for work, there is now a whole checklist of things you must have in place.

You will need to:

- Obtain Basic STCW Safety qualifications, which include: Personal Survival Techniques, Fire Fighting, First Aid, Personal Safety & Social Responsibility, Elementary First Aid, and Proficiency of Security Awareness.
- Hold a valid ENG 1 Medical certificate.
- Complete advanced crew agency registration online.
- Write a good quality CV.

Of course, you'll also need to decide which type of crew job is right for you.

What position do you want to apply for?

Yachting is an industry with a very clear hierarchy. The chart below will give you an idea of the roles involved and how they all fit together.

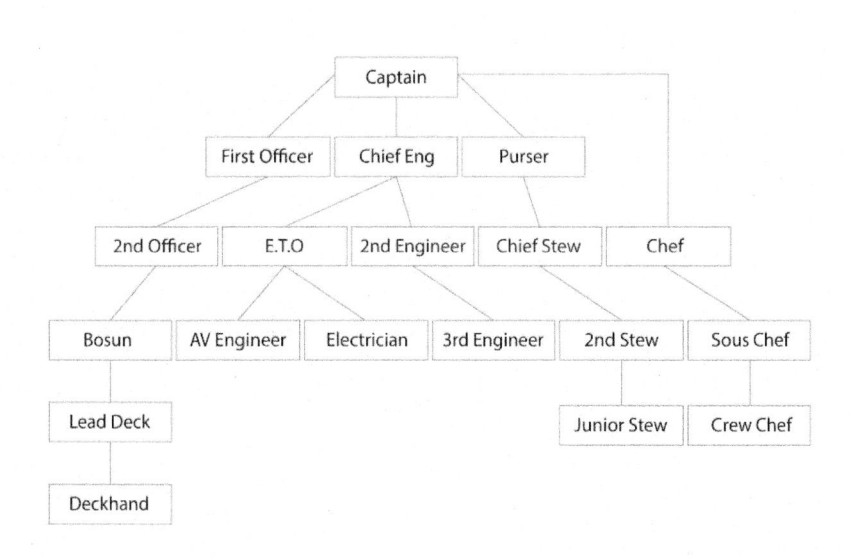

```
                            Captain
              ┌───────────────┼───────────────┐
         First Officer    Chief Eng         Purser
       ┌──────┬───────┬──────┼──────┬──────────┐
   2nd Officer  E.T.O    2nd Engineer  Chief Stew    Chef
       │     ┌──┴──┬──────┐       ┌──────┬──────┐
     Bosun  AV Eng Electrician 3rd Eng  2nd Stew  Sous Chef
       │                                   │         │
   Lead Deck                          Junior Stew  Crew Chef
       │
    Deckhand
```

45

If you're new to the industry, you will likely start in a junior role no matter how old you are. This is often the case even if you have worked in a similar industry previously, though there is sometimes some flexibility. If you have relevant qualifications or transferable skills you *may* be able to come in at a higher level. Alternatively, you're likely to find that you still need to start in a junior role but could possibly advance through the ranks more quickly.

The Deck Team

The Captain directly manages the deck team. He or she and their senior team members are responsible for the safe navigation of the vessel. The rest of the deck team are responsible for the maintenance and upkeep of the exterior of the yacht. It's their job to ensure it's always in pristine condition.

The deck team also look after all tenders and toys. This means that as part of their role, they are expected to take guests out on water sport activities and be involved with beach set-ups. This is a two-part role: they need to make sure guests are well entertained while also keeping them safe at all times.

It is the deck team who look after the onboard safety procedures. This involves providing safety briefings regarding boat issues, conducting drills, and providing safety training for the crew.

Deckhand

Day-to-day duties include:

- Cleaning and maintenance of the exterior of the vessel, including washing down, polishing, waxing, sanding, painting and varnishing
- Tender driving
- Looking after water sports equipment
- Running water sports activities such as such as water skiing, wake boarding, kite surfing, and jet skis
- Line handling

Skills required:

- STCW Basic Safety Training

- ENG1/ML 5 Medical Fitness Certificate
- Powerboat level 2

Make your CV stand out from the crowd with transferable skills in areas such as carpentry, painting, varnishing, boat building, and water sports. Any experience or training in these areas will help you to secure your first position.

Lead Deckhand

Day-to-day duties include:

- All entry level deckhand duties
- Training new deck crew
- Overseeing junior deck crew

Skills required:

- Prior experience as a deckhand
- Ability to teach a variety of water sports
- Confident tender driver
- Hold a Yachtmaster Offshore qualification (or be working towards it)
- Knowledge of cleaning and maintenance products

Bosun (found on larger vessels)

Day-to-day duties include:

- Looking after the deckhands
- Overseeing daily duties for the team
- Navigation and standing watch
- Executing planned maintenance

Skills required:

- Yachtmaster Offshore qualification
- Some vessels require the Bosun to be working towards OOW tickets
- Prior experience as a deckhand
- Ability to teach a variety of water sports
- Confident tender driver in both night and day conditions
- Knowledge of products and strong maintenance skills
- Good leadership skills

Second Officer / Officer of the Watch (found on larger vessels)

Day-to-day duties include:

- Assisting the First Officer with implementing deck maintenance plan
- Administrative duties
- Assisting with safety procedures on board

- Navigational watch

Skills required:

- Previous experience as a Deckhand and Bosun
- Hold OOW ticket and continuing deck studies
- Up-to-date knowledge of all products and repair procedures
- Strong leadership skills
- Extensive water sports knowledge and experience

First Officer (Chief Officer, Chief Mate)

Day-to-day duties include:

- Second in command to the captain
- Direct management of the deck crew and yacht exterior
- Assisting with the navigation and passage planning
- Undertaking bridge watches
- Gaining more drive time experience
- Ensuring the safety of the yacht, the yacht crew, and guests on board
- Overseeing deck operations and maintenance programs
- Overseeing the deck crew
- Supervising guest recreational activities
- Maintaining records of safety inspections and crew certifications
- Implementing safety procedures on board

- Carrying out various safety drills
- Setting watch schedules
- Potentially acting as medical officer or designated security person

Skills required:

- Good Navigation skills
- Boat handling
- Knowledge of international maritime law
- Extensive knowledge and experience of deck maintenance
- Management and leadership skills
- Safety knowledge
- Either a Chief Mate 3000gt ticket, MCA STCW Officer of the Watch, or usually on smaller yachts, the Yachtmaster Ocean certificate. Merchant Navy certifications are also recognised
- Exceptional ISM & ISPS knowledge
- A good understanding of engineering
- Experience of working to budgets
- Strong leadership skills/ability to delegate and give clear instructions

Captain

Day-to-day duties include:

- The safe navigation and operation of the yacht

- Full charge and overall responsibility of the vessel
- All department heads report directly to the captain
- Responsible for liaising directly with the owner with regards to their requirements and any decisions that need to be made
- Must ensure that owners' expectations are met at all times
- Hiring and firing of crew members
- Project management
- Budgeting and accounting issues

Skills required:

- Considerable years of training and experience
- Navigation and yacht operations
- Good cruising knowledge of a wide range of areas
- Strong knowledge and understanding of maritime law
- Extensive experience of personnel management
- Experience of shipyard and project management
- Very good understanding of accounting
- Calm and charismatic personality
- Excellent leadership and communication skills
- Great people skills
- Exceptional ISM & ISPS knowledge
- Thorough understanding of health and safety expectations
- Excellent engineering knowledge and the ability to troubleshoot
- Qualifications depend on the vessel

The Engineering Team

Engineers are the heart and soul of any yacht. Their main responsibilities are for the maintenance and servicing of every piece of mechanical and electrical equipment on a yacht.

Their responsibility covers the safety of the vessel through firefighting and alarm systems, the efficiency of the boat and pollution prevention. From the main engines and generators, to toilets, water production, fixing toasters and kettles, to all audio-visual and IT equipment. Yachting engineers need to be extremely confident in their technical abilities.

The engineering team also has a duty to educate the crew on technical and safety related issues.

Junior Engineer

Day-to-day duties include:
- Cleaning and detailing the engine room
- Working with and learning from more senior engineers
- Basic maintenance such as replacing light bulbs
- Basic repairs
- Ensuring that there is enough water in the tanks for guests and crew to take showers
- Basic engine maintenance
- Solving internet and TV problems

You will have a willingness to learn about, and take care of everything from replacing light bulbs to fixing a broken toaster; to making sure there is enough water in the tanks for the guests and crew to be able to take a shower, basic engine maintenance, to solving any Internet and IT problems. There will be lots of cleaning and detailing of the engine room too.

Skills required:
- Enthusiasm and willingness to learn
- AEC
- Basic STCW & PSA
- ENG 1

Make your CV stand out from the crowd with transferable skills such as marine engineering or motor mechanic, plumbing, electrician.

2nd Engineer

Day-to-day duties include:

- Maintenance and repairs
- Working very closely with the chief engineer
- Assisting the chief to ensure smooth running of engine room operations
- Directing the engineering team
- Carrying out daily logs and system checks
- Keeping track of planned maintenance
- Deciding with the chief which tasks to address each day
- Training junior engineers

Skills required:

- Good prior experience in the engine room
- Excellent technical and troubleshooting experience
- Ability to prioritise
- Advanced knowledge of all on board systems
- Ability to train junior staff and show leadership skills
- Be technically minded
- Be well-briefed on safety aspects of the vessel such as firefighting,

- isolations and pump, operations, safety training, and pollution prevention
- Required qualifications depend on the size of the vessel and could vary from an AEC all the way up to a Y1 ticket.

Chief Engineer

Day-to-day duties include:

- Managing the engineering department and answering to the captain
- Taking responsibility for the safe working order of every piece of machinery on board
- Ensuring the safety of all engine room operations
- Maintenance and repairs
- Managing a team of engineers (unless it is a very small boat, in which case the chief engineer may be the sole engineer on board)
- Executing planned maintenance programs and carrying out preventative maintenance
- Completing administration and paperwork for the department
- Ordering parts in from local ports
- Securing and project managing outside contractors

Skills required:

- Extensive technical knowledge

- A great deal of experience working on yacht engines, generators, drive systems, water-makers, electrical systems, air conditioning units, tenders, and jet-skis
- Good leadership skills
- Ability to delegate, manage, and supervise
- An understanding of ISM
- Qualifications as dictated by the size of the vessel and their individual safe manning requirements

Electrical Technical Officer (ETO)

This role is normally found on larger super yachts that have a big team of engineers.

Day-to-day duties include:

- Responsibility for all electrical equipment such as computers, GPS, navigational equipment, TVs and internet connections
- General electrical maintenance and repairs

Skills required:
- Prior experience with AV/IT equipment
- Preferably a qualification in electronics
- Training in computer repairs, televisions, internet, radar and navigation equipment, and communication equipment such as satellites, phones, and radios

- STCW basic crew training
- ENG1/ML 5 Medical Fitness Certificate
- MCA Engineering certification

The Interior Team

The interior team provides a seven-star service with a big smile (yes, always!). They ensure that all guests and crew areas are flawlessly clean and tidy. Their responsibilities include looking after laundry and wardrobe, providing a food and drink service, providing clean linens and towels, the provisioning of guest toiletries and sundry items, cocktail making, flower arranging, cleaning and, most importantly, making sure that all guests are happy and have their every need catered to.

Junior Steward/ess

Day-to-day duties include:
- Cleaning and maintaining the appearance and upkeep of the interior of the boat, both guest and crew areas
- Following orders from the senior interior staff
- Providing a turn down service for guests
- Laundry, stain removal, and fabric care
- Ironing
- Food and drink service (this may include fine dining or silver service, depending on the requirements of the guests and set up of the interior department)
- Bar tending
- Barista
- Flower arranging and plant care
- Assisting the chief stewardess with other duties such as provisioning of guest and crew items such as toiletries, towels, and linens

Skills required:
- Enthusiasm and willingness to learn
- Basic STCW training & PSA
- Food safety and hygiene certification
- ENG 1
- Good administration and computer skills

Make your CV stand out from the crowd with previous experience in hospitality such as: working in hotels, waitressing, bar tending, barista, floristry, or working in a private house as a housekeeper.

Extra training such as the Stewardess interior training courses or the PYA Guest courses can be helpful, although these are not mandatory.

2nd Steward/ess

Day-to-day duties include:
- Working closely with the chief steward/ess
- Implementing and executing the work list with the rest of the interior team
- Training junior stewardesses
- Taking on the chief stewardess role in their absence
- Cleaning and maintaining the interior of the boat
- Food and drink service
- Overseeing and assisting with laundry

Skills required:
- Two or more years of industry experience (depending on vessel requirements)
- Strong service, housekeeping, and laundry skills
- Good attention to detail
- Ability to delegate and manage a team
- Experience with boat stowage and inventories

- Knowledge of glassware and tableware
- Napkin folding and table setting skills
- Cocktail making and barista skills
- Strong awareness of what makes good service
- Excellent people skills

Chief Steward/ess

Day-to-day duties include:
- Managing the interior team
- Answering to the captain
- Managing interior maintenance and repairs
- Arranging rotas for service and housekeeping
- Interior project management
- Responsibility for overall service, laundry, and housekeeping procedures
- Planning guest entertainment including themed nights, beach days, and events
- Liaising with guests as to their meal and drink requirements as well as their desired daily activities
- Provisioning for guest supplies
- Protecting and caring for valuable items such as art work, marble, china, and crystal
- Accounting and budgeting for the department
- Managing all interior inventories
- Responsibility for crew uniform management and ordering

- Motivating and training the interior team

Skills required:
- Several years industry experience
- Strong management and leadership skills
- Ability to delegate
- Excellent service and housekeeping skills
- Vast knowledge of wine, spirits, and cigars
- Understanding of cruising areas and activities
- Knowledge of flower arranging and plant care
- Strong computer and administrative skills
- Excellent communication skills
- Exceptional organisational skills
- Impressive attention to detail

On very large yachts, the interior department may be split into two departments: Housekeeping and Service. In this case, each department will have a manager.

Purser

Yachts of a certain size may require a Purser to manage the interior and finances on board.

Day-to-day duties include:
- Assisting the Captain with PA and legalities

- Accounting
- Crew contracts and documentation
- Purchasing
- Provisioning

Skills required:

- Extensive interior team experience, usually two or more years in a chief steward/ess position
- Good understanding of maritime law
- Knowledge of ISM & ISPS protocols
- Knowledge of cruising areas, including restaurant suggestions and shore side activities
- Experience provisioning around the globe
- Excellent knowledge of wines, spirits, and cigars
- Impeccable service skills
- Strong computer skills and knowledge

The Galley Team

The galley is where you will find the chef. Depending on the size of the yacht, the chef will either work alone or as part of a team. Bigger vessels will employ a Crew Chef, Sous Chef, Head Chef.

The galley team cooks for both guests and crew. They are also responsible for provisioning food and looking after all stocks in the fridges, freezers, and dry stores on board. Positions in this department can be incredibly stressful as meal plans, guest requirements, and the number of guests eating can all change at very short notice.

Yacht chefs normally come from a restaurant background and have a good, well-rounded knowledge of a variety of world cuisines. They will also need to have an awareness of dietary requirements and have a finger on the pulse of the latest dieting trends.

Chefs can work long hours; they are often up very early to prepare breakfast before the guests awake. They then need to cook, provision, and maintain a pristine galley throughout the day and evening while also preparing trays of canapés and snacks to satisfy any partying guests who wish to stay up late.

Crew Cook

On larger yachts, you will find a Crew Cook who has a dedicated responsibility to cook for the crew.

Day-to-day duties include:
- Preparing all meals for the crew
- Assisting the main chef and their team when required
- Catering for dietary requirements
- Provisioning for crew meals and food stores in the crew mess areas
- Possibly assisting with deck or interior duties when required

Skills required:

- Food safety and hygiene certification
- Formal qualifications aren't mandatory, but most cooks do have a relevant qualification or prior restaurant experience as a cook
- Ability to provision
- Knowledge of and enthusiasm for food and produce
- A good understanding of nutrition
- Strong awareness of allergies and dietary requirements
- Awareness of the latest dieting trends

Sous Chef

Day-to-day duties include:
- Supporting and answerable to the Head Chef
- Provisioning
- Maintaining stocks
- Tracking inventories
- Cooking for the crew while the Head Chef focuses on guest meals
- Assisting with guest meals as directed
- Detailing and maintaining the galley to a high level of cleanliness

Skills required:
- Prior experience as a chef in a restaurant
- Food safety and hygiene certification
- A knowledge of and enthusiasm for food and produce
- A good understanding of nutrition
- A strong awareness of allergies and dietary requirements
- Ability to effectively provision
- An awareness of the latest dieting trends

Head Chef

Day-to-day duties:
- Preparing all meals for guests
- The provisioning of all food items, wherever the vessel is in the world

- Menu planning
- Food preparation
- Overall responsibility for food safety and storage
- Working within a budget
- Managing the Galley team
- Presenting guest food to an exceptional level
- Bringing creative flair to onboard food

- <u>Skills required:</u>
- Prior experience as a chef on a yacht and in a restaurant environment
- Culinary trained
- Food safety and hygiene certification
- Experience of working to budgets
- Knowledge of world cuisines
- Experience of provisioning worldwide
- Excellent presentation skills
- Ability to plan impressive menus
- Accounting and computer skills
- Highly organised and able to work to tight time constraints

Cook/Sole Chef

On smaller vessels there is typically one cook. In these cases, they can also be known as a sole chef.

Day-to-day duties:

- Preparing all meals for owners, guests and crew
- Provisioning all food items for the kitchen, bar and the crew mess
- Menu planning and preparation
- Working to food safety requirements
- Catering to dietary needs
- Working to budgets
- Cooks on very small yachts will normally be expected to assist the deck and/or interior teams

Skills required:

- Food safety and hygiene certification
- Formal qualifications aren't mandatory, but most cooks do have a relevant qualification
- Prior restaurant experience as a cook
- Ability to provision
- Knowledge of and enthusiasm for food and produce
- A good understanding of nutrition
- Strong awareness of allergies and dietary requirements
- Awareness of the latest dieting trends

Combined and Specialist Roles

Some yachts advertise positions for combined roles. This may be because it is a smaller yacht, and crew members will all be expected to take on two positions. Alternatively, in some cases, this is because the yacht has a requirement for a special skill. If you have any relevant additional qualifications or skills, it could make you a much more desirable candidate.

What additional skills could be beneficial? Below are a few examples.

If you are looking to become a **steward/ess** complimentary skills and qualifications include: massage therapy, beauty therapy, hairdressing, personal training, cooking, yoga instructing, nanny, or even nursing.

It's a big benefit for a **deckhand** to have prior experience teaching water sports or sailing, or to hold instructor certificates, for example, kite surfing, PWC (jet ski) instructing, or anything particularly specialist in this area. Additionally, any prior tradesman skills such as carpentry, plumbing, electrical, woodwork, or boat building can majorly increase your hire-ability factor!

Those who are looking to step into an **engineering** role for the first time may find this is possible thanks to their previous career. If you have experience in marine engineering, mechanical engineering, electrical engineering, or plumbing, or if you have prior experience working in any capacity on deck, whether that be dive boats, fishing, or cruise ships, then a combined deck/engineering role could help you secure a position.

Want to work in the **galley**? Prior kitchen experience in a high-end establishment would give your CV a great boost. If you don't have this, you could make use of any prior hospitality or sailing experience to make you a more desirable candidate for a combined galley role such as Cook/Steward/ess or Deck/Cook.

It's important to note that the individuals who apply for these combined roles will almost always be expected to take on more traditional yachting duties alongside their specialist work.

For example, if a yacht is looking for a massage therapist, this will normally be combined with a steward/ess role. As your massage skills will only be required when the boat is in guest mode, the rest of the time you would resume your role as a steward/ess assisting with laundry and housekeeping.

Other specialist roles

From time to time yachts do advertise for other specialist roles. These could include:

- Personal trainers
- Yoga instructors
- Beauty therapists
- Massage therapists
- Hairdressers
- Dive instructors
- Water sports instructors
- Florists
- Helicopter pilots
- Security officers
- Nannies
- Tutors
- Sommeliers
- Fishing experts
- Carpenters
- Butlers
- Estate managers

Mia's Seafarer Story

Mia is an Australian 2nd Stewardess with four years' experience. She started out in the Yachting industry at the age of 20 after her UK visa ran out. She wasn't quite ready to go home yet, so she took to the water instead.

There's an awful lot of hard work involved in yachting, but there are also some really good times to be had! The first three yachts I worked on were extremely fun. We travelled all through Greece, Turkey, France, and Italy. I got on really well with our owners, and because of this, there was a lot of guest/crew interaction. This led to some amazing experiences: partying in Monaco with the owner and his friends, going on snorkelling trips and finding sunken tenders in Greece, and hiking in Turkey. I had the time of my life.

After this, I decided I wanted to really achieve something out of my career, and I started to look for a larger charter boat to work on while I saved up to buy a house back in Australia. I'm happy to report that I found my yacht, and after a lot of hard work on board, I found my house too!

If I were to start in the industry all over again, I would probably aim to start on a larger yacht and work down in size. Larger yachts are a lot more formal in structure. On a smaller yacht, you have more of a life, and your interactions with the guests are very different. In my experience, on a smaller yacht, crew and guests are more like family!

I am forever grateful that I discovered yachting. It is an amazing industry, and I couldn't be in a happier position. Thanks to this job, I have made some of the best friends I've ever had, explored places I never knew existed, and become the cleanest person ever!

It does take a lot to be a successful yachtie. The first time I was told to detail a cabin with a Q-tip (cotton bud) my jaw just about hit the ground! Despite this, A LOT of people think I sail around the world in my bikini, possibly because I don't post pictures of me cleaning toilets on Facebook. Little do they know you stand on your feet for countless hours, you're away from your family and friends, and that you basically clean for a living.

Chapter Five

What to expect from your yachting contract

In most ways, a yachting career will be considerably different from any other you may have had before. However, many usual career considerations still apply!

Before you start job hunting, it's a good idea to familiarise yourself with what you can expect in terms of salary and employment contract.

Salary guidelines

Salaries can vary depending on the size of the boat, if it's private or charter, if your role is rotational and on individual budgets. Also, keep in mind that not all positions are available on all size boats. The tables in this section will give you an indication of what you might be able to expect to be paid per month. All monthly salaries are a guide only and are given in Euros.

Deck team

	20-30m	30-45m	45-60m	60-80m	80m+
Deckhand	1800 - 2500€ p/m	2000-2500€ p/m	2000-3000€ p/m	2000-3500€ p/m	2500+€ p/m
Bosun	N/a	N/a	3500 - 4500€ p/m	3500 - 5000€ p/m	5000+€ p/m
2nd Mate	N/a	N/a	4000-4500€ p/m	4000-5000€ p/m	6000+€ p/m
First Mate	2500-3000€ p/m	3000 - 4500€ p/m	4000-6000€ p/m	5000-7000€ p/m	8000+€ p/m
Captain	3500-5500€ p/m	5000 - 8000€ p/m	8000-11,000€ p/m	11,000-13,000€ p/m	13,000+€ p/m

Engineering team

	20 - 30m	30-45m	45-60m	60m – 80m	80m+
Junior Engineer	N/a	N/a	2500-3500€ p/m	2500-4000€ p/m	2500+€ p/m
2nd Engineer	N/a	N/a	4500-6000€ p/m	5500-7500€ p/m	7500+€ p/m
Chief Engineer	3500-4000€ p/m	3000-5500€ p/m	5000-9000€ p/m	7000-10,000€ p/m	10,000+€ p/m

Interior team

	20 - 30m	30-45m	45-60m	60 - 80m	80m+
Steward/ess	1800-2500€ p/m	1800-2500€ p/m	2000-3000€ p/m	2500-3000€ p/m	2500-3000€ p/m
2nd Stew/ess	N/a	2000-3000€ p/m	2500-4000€ p/m	3500-5000€ p/m	4500+€ p/m
Chief Steward/ess	3000€ p/m	3000-4500€ p/m	4000-6000€ p/m	5000-7000€ p/m	7000+€ p/m

Galley team

	20 - 30m	30-45m	45 -60m	60-80m	80m+
Crew/Sous Chef	N/a	N/a	2500-4500€ p/m	3500-6000€ p/m	5500+€ p/m
Chef	3000-4000€ p/m	4000-4500€ p/m	5000-7000€ p/m	6000+€ p/m	8000+€ p/m

Types of contract and terms of employment

Not all yachting contracts are created equal. There are numerous different types of positions you could be offered. These include permanent, rotational, seasonal, relief (temp), and day work.

You may want to keep in mind that the salaries, bonuses, and benefits on offer are not comparable to any land-based industry. Many yachts offer benefit packages that include things such as health insurance, dental insurance, flight allowances, and educational allowances.

In return, you should be asked to sign a SEA (Seafarers Employment Agreement) or crew contract, and possibly a non-disclosure agreement.

What to expect from a permanent contract

A full time permanent employment contract will normally give you annual paid holiday of between 4-8 weeks per annum. Permanent crew members are typically paid on a monthly basis and are sometimes given a thirteenth-month bonus after a year of service. Overtime is rarely compensated for; rather, it's expected. However, if you are on a charter yacht, you can normally receive guest tips on top of your salary.

Depending on your yachts' policy, you can sometimes be given an education allowance. This can be really helpful if you are trying to work your way through the ranks as it means your employer will cover the cost of gaining any necessary qualifications. Do check your contract terms carefully, though, as if you leave within a year of completing any courses or training, you may be required to pay back a percentage of any education allowance you've received.

What to expect from a seasonal contract

Seasonal employment is when you work on a contract that's written to cover the period when the yacht is in owner or charter mode. The dates of 'the season' vary for each particular vessel, and the part of the world in which they are based. Depending on the demands of owners and/or charter guests, a typical seasonal contract can run from anything between three and six months.

What to expect from a rotational contact

As you work your way through the ranks and move up to more senior roles, some yachts will offer rotational contracts. These are often sought after as they offer much more time off than traditional contracts. If you have a rotational contract, you will work a set period on board before having a set period of leave; perhaps two months on the yacht followed by two months leave. Whether or not this time off is paid will depend on your contract.

Historically rotational contracts were offered for Captains, First Officers, Engineers, and Pursers, and to date have been almost non-existent for junior roles. However, there is good news, the industry is changing. More and more larger yachts are starting to offer rotations such as 3 months on, 1 month off rotation for more junior roles; this has affected the salaries a little bit as more time off has meant a slight decrease in monthly wage to compensate the extra time off.

What to expect from a freelance/temp contract

Yachts frequently offer work on a freelance or temporary basis. This is normally to cover a crew member who is off sick, on holiday, or on leave for a personal emergency. Freelance and temp staff are also commonly used during periods when there are lots of guests on board and the crew needs an additional pair of hands. Though work on this basis often doesn't come with many employment benefits, taking it can be a really good way to build experience and make contacts. Also, a temp job is the best way to find out if you're really cut out for the yachtie lifestyle!

What to expect from a day work

Day work is just what it says on the tin... sort of. A day worker would normally live on land and comes to work on the boat for the day. This type of staff member is often employed during periods in the yard, or to assist with getting the boat ready for owner and guest arrivals. Day work can be literally just for one day, or it could be for a week to a couple of months. A day worker does not have any of the benefits of a fully employed crew member; they will be paid a daily rate.

What to expect from a delivery contract

The nature of yachts means that they sometimes need to be delivered from one port to another. A yacht that is being delivered in this way will require a crew to get them there. A delivery contract means that you are employed during this delivery period, which could be anything from a few days to a month or more depending on the distance involved. Once the boat has been delivered, and your work is done, you will disembark.

What to expect from a yard period contract

Sometimes extra staff or contractors are required while a yacht is in the shipyard. When a yacht is in the shipyard, a range of repair works, small and large, will be carried out. This could be anything from engine repairs, interior refits, and exterior paint jobs. The nature of the work that's needed will dictate how long a boat is in the shipyard. Sometimes this is a few days, but a yard period can also last for many, many months! If there is a lot to be done, the boat will often employ extra staff to see them through this period and may even house them in an apartment on shore.

What else do you need to know about yachting contracts?

Hours of work

I've already spoken about a typical onboard working schedule so you'll know that your hours of work are likely to be long and changeable. Yachts that comply with the Maritime Labour Convention (MLC) should legally give crew eight hours of rest between shifts.

Most onboard work will be done in shift patterns. Your usual hours of work could vary between day shifts, swing shifts (late start/late finish), night shifts, or split shifts (which is part day and part evening with an extended break in the middle).

You may find that your usual sleeping patterns change dramatically during your time on board! This is particularly likely if you are a member of the engineering or deck crew as someone from these teams will usually have to be on duty twenty-four hours a day. This could mean doing a first shift from midnight till 4am, then a second from noon until 6pm. In order to get a reasonable amount of sleep on a shift pattern like this, you would need to go to bed twice in a day.

Holiday entitlement

Individual yachts have their own policy and individual annual holiday entitlement typically falls between four and eight weeks per annum. If you're really lucky there are yachts out there that offer up to three months.

Holiday entitlement can sometimes include an allowance for travel. This can take the form of the cost of a flight or two per year. For example, if you're from the UK and the boat is in Florida when you want to take your time off, on some contracts, the cost of this airfare will be covered by the yacht.

Additional benefits

Working on a yacht certainly means a lot less time off than more traditional employment, but the industry does work hard to counteract this with some of the other benefits it offers. It's worth remembering that you will have no accommodation or food expenses. Many yachting contracts also include added benefits such as education allowances; private healthcare and private dental plans.

Joel's Seafarer Story

Joel is a 2nd Engineer on board a super yacht. He's been in the yachting industry for twelve years and previously worked for more than twenty years as a Marine Engineer. He's thinking of retiring soon!

Picture this: I'm a 2nd Engineer on a privately owned 80m motor yacht with a crew of twenty-four. The boat alternates between the Mediterranean for the summer and the Caribbean for the winter.

I'll start off by saying that there's no such thing as a typical day in the life of an engineer! Every day is different, but here's an example of what might happen on a day when the boat is in port on standby for the owner's pleasure.

I start work at 8am. The engineering teams assemble in the Engine Control Room (ECR) to have a brief chat about the boat's status for that day. After this, I check out the planned maintenance system and plan my day to accommodate what needs to be done. Then I brief the 3rd engineer on the day's plan of attack, as well as dealing with any ongoing repairs or failures.

First up: completing the Engineering Log. This is a detailed matrix of facts and figures concerning every piece of equipment that has something that will affect its operation; an oil level, a temperature, a pressure, an RPM, or a voltage. This log is completed every 24 hours.

The rest of today's jobs:

Monthly greasing of the forward crane, including testing all safety stops and limits and inspecting the lifting cable and hook mechanism

- *Monthly cleansing of sight glass in the Ultraviolet (UV) steriliser*
- *Weekly fire and safety checks: testing emergency lighting, sprinkler system test functions, and fire alarm system test functions.*
- *De-sludge and clean the DVZ system (sewage treatment plant)*
- *Service the 250-hour Centre Generator*

Of course, the unexpected always plays a part. As well as these planned tasks, I also need to deal with anything else that comes up. Today:

1. *A crew cabin toilet won't flush.*
2. *A lorry load of spares has arrived and needs to be checked and entered into inventory.*
3. *A bilge float switch in a tender needs repairing.*
4. *A belt on an air-conditioning air handler needs adjusting.*
5. *The passarelle has broken.*

I usually squeeze in a few breaks during 8am and 5pm: breakfast from 09.30-10:00, lunch from 12:30-13:30, and afternoon tea from 15:00-15:30. However, if any critical equipment is out of service, everything else goes out of the window until the problem is resolved.

Chapter Six

Training and qualifications

It's time to talk qualifications!

The first step to being taken seriously in this industry is to invest in your yachting education.

Yachting is full of fly-by-nights, backpackers, gap-year students, and people looking to make fast money, but the majority of employers are looking for crew who want to make a career out of yachting.

Training courses may seem like a hefty expense to pay before you even get started, but investing now will make you a much more desirable candidate and will show how committed you are to the industry.

Not sure where you should start? In the next section, I've set out the basic requirements for all new and prospective crew members.

STCW Basic Safety Training

Whatever crew position you're applying for, the STCW Basic Safety Training is the minimum requirement to step on board a yacht.

STCW stands for **Standards of Training, Certification and Watchkeeping.**

This is entry-level certification is offered in maritime schools all over the globe and takes five and a half days to complete. Costs vary depending on the location of the school, but the average is £850 or around €1200.

The course consists of five modules:

1. Personal Survival Techniques

During this training, you will learn what to do to ensure your survival in the event that you have to abandon ship at sea. This includes the preparations you should make, as well as pool drills that cover the correct use of an inflatable life raft, boarding, capsizing, and rescue.

2. Fire Fighting

The implications of a fire on board can be drastic, particularly at sea when assistance is rarely nearby. It's therefore very important for yachts to have well-trained and competent crew who can deal with real-life fire situations. This module covers all the basics such as fire prevention, firefighting skills, causes of fires aboard ships, and how to deal with a fire safely and efficiently.

3. Elementary First Aid

This section of the course will teach you what to do if you encounter any medical emergencies on board. You'll learn how to treat burns and scalds, bleeding, shock, and broken bones. This module also covers bandaging methods, how to move and position a patient, resuscitation, and how to improvise with various materials you may find on board.

4. Personal Safety & Social Responsibility (PSSR)

This covers important knowledge for any crew member and includes all you need to know about issues including personal safety procedures, employment rights, sexual harassment, pollution prevention, the effects of drug abuse, relations with others on board, responses to emergencies, and onboard organisation.

5. Proficiency in Security Awareness (PSA)

This is the newest module in the course and *not all training schools include it in their course cost; it can be an added extra.* Make sure you double-check this when you are researching where to complete the course. This is important as any commercially registered yacht you apply to will require you to have completed this module.

This module is designed to meet the requirements for training set out in the International Ship and Port Facility Security Code (ISPS Code) and the guidance laid out in the SOLAS Regulations 1974. It has become mandatory for new and existing crew unless they already hold SSO (ships security officer) or PDSD (proficiency in designated security duties) license.

It includes operational requirement of the ISPS code, ship security arrangements, methods of personal search and ship search, security surveillance, and how to response to a security incident.

Proficiency in Designated Security Duties (PDSD)

This course is the next level up from the Proficiency in Security Awareness (PSA) included in most STCW Basic Safety Training courses. If you do this course, you do *not* need to have completed the PSA module as this will be covered again in the PDSD.

The full course title is the **MCA Accredited STCW ISPS Proficiency in Designated Security Duties (PDSD)**. It covers the knowledge, understanding, and proficiency requirements set out in the STCW Convention and Code 1978. The PDSD Course has been designed to give crew, who will have designated security duties under the ships security plan, an understanding of the various security responsibilities and knowledge of the Ship Maritime Security Levels. The PDSD course also incorporates Anti-Piracy Awareness Training.

This course content includes:

- Recognising security risks and threats
- Security systems and equipment
- ISPS code overview
- Circumvention of security
- Relevant international codes and conventions
- Ship security plan
- Ship security assessment
- Handling of stowaways and refugees
- Introduction to improvised explosive devices

ENG 1 Medical

This isn't a course, but it is a recommended requirement for all yachting industry crew. It is a seafarer's medical, which consists of a brief physical exam, blood pressure measurements, measurement of BMI, a sight test, a colour blindness test, and a hearing test. It costs around £80/120€ depending on where you are located. Many yachts will require you to have the certificate before they hire you.

It's important to know that there aren't many doctors who can provide this certificate. You won't just be able to ask your normal GP. There are, however, doctors all over the world who are approved to do this, so start looking for one based near you *before* you apply for any jobs. The waiting list to get an appointment with approved doctors in Antibes and other yachting hubs can be as long as three weeks during high season. If you leave it to the last minute, it could mean that you miss out on a possible job opportunity.

The UK government provides lists of MCA-approved doctors based both in the UK and overseas. They can be found by visiting:

https://www.gov.uk/government/publications/mca-approved-doctors-uk-based — for UK based doctors.

https://www.gov.uk/government/uploads/system/uploads/attachment_data/file/320980/140613_MCA_Approved_Doctors_Overseas.pdf — for doctors based overseas.

What other industry training courses do you need to know about?

It's a good idea to look into additional courses that may benefit your chosen career path. Making an investment in your future career now will help you to be taken more seriously when applying for positions. Relevant courses can also be a real boost to your CV if you don't have any previous related experience.

Any additional courses you choose to take will be specific to the career path you plan to follow. Most won't be available to you until you have actually started in the industry, but researching them in advance will give you a good indication of what you will need to do to progress in your chosen yachting career.

General training courses

Level 2 - Food Hygiene and Safety Course

Under UK & European law, **every person who handles food or drinks** in a commercial capacity must hold a food hygiene and safety qualification. This applies on any MLC-compliant yacht. All members of the interior team will, therefore, need to complete a food safety course, as will any crew members from the exterior team who are ever called in to assist with service.

This qualification is only required on commercial yachts, but I'd say it's still worthwhile obtaining it in advance even if you plan to work on a private vessel. Once you've been certified, you'll be prepared should you ever be offered a job on a commercial yacht.

This qualification can be done online through The Virtual College of Food Safety (whose online courses have been approved by the MCA), but in order to get the full qualification, you will need to be assessed at an accredited test centre.

Course content includes:

- Introduction to food safety
- Refrigeration, chilling, and cold holding of foods
- Cooking, hot holding, and re-heating of foods
- Food handling

- Principles of safe food storage
- Cleaning
- Food safety and hygiene law
- Food safety hazards

If you have previously worked in hospitality, you may already hold a valid certificate. You can check if your existing qualification is valid by visiting the UK government's list of recognised qualifications at **https://www.gov.uk/**

Training courses for the deck department

Powerboat Level 2

The PBL2 is a two-day course that covers the skills needed to drive a small tender or rigid inflatable boat up of up to ten metres in length. It is required by law to have this license when operating a tender in Mediterranean waters. No previous experience is necessary to complete this course.

Course content includes:
- Basic boat handling
- Collision avoidance
- High-speed manoeuvres
- Man overboard procedures

Tender Operator Licence

This is another two-day course that's designed with safety in mind to give power boaters some advanced training on navigation both for during the day and (more importantly) at night. There are a couple of pre-requisites for this training course. You must be seventeen or over, and you must already hold the PBL2, a First Aid Certificate, and VHF Radio Certificates.

Course content includes:

- Passenger safety and comfort
- Emergency situations
- Associated theory

Jet Ski License (PWC)

This is a one-day course that will suit both first-time Jet Ski riders and those with previous Jet Ski experience who wish to operate a personal watercraft.

New regulations in the Mediterranean mean that if you want to ride a Jet Ski, you must present the appropriate Jet Ski license (known as a Personal Watercraft Certificate) to the authorities. No previous experience is needed to complete this course.

Course content includes:

- Launching and recovery

- Safety on the water
- Navigation
- High-speed Jet Ski handling

Personal Water Craft Instructor (PWI)

Most large motorboats and super yachts carry jet skis for the entertainment of their guests. All maritime administrations in the Mediterranean require Jet Ski operators to be licensed. The Royal Yachting Association (RYA) has developed clear standards for the operation of personal watercrafts (Jet Skis), including the rule that if a yacht carries Jets Skis, it must employ a qualified RYA PWC Instructor.

This rule means that there is high demand for yacht crew who hold the PWC Instructor certificate. If you are looking for work in the industry, particularly in the deck team, gaining the RYA PWC Instructor certificate will greatly enhance your chances of employment.

There are some prerequisites for this course. You'll need to have previous Jet Ski experience, a PWC competency license, a valid first aid certificate, and you will need to become a registered member of the RYA in order for you to qualify as an RYA Instructor.

Course content includes:
- Practice and observe teaching styles
- Course programming and management

- Session planning
- The role of the instructor
- The use of visual aids
- Teaching sessions

Mega Yacht Deck Crew Course

This is a five-day course that requires no previous experience or qualifications. It isn't mandatory, but can be a good way to ensure your CV stands out against those of other deck team hopefuls. The course covers both the theory and practical aspects of basic seamanship and exterior deck duties.

Course content includes
- On board safety policies
- Onboard safety equipment
- Lines and knots
- Collision regulations
- Introduction to VHF radio operation

Yacht Rating

The Yacht Rating is a qualification gained through experience and sea time.

In order to qualify, you will need to have six months yacht service, two months sea service, STCW basic safety training certificate, the ENG1 seaman's medical certificate, and a completed Yacht Rating Training Record Book.

For more information on the Yacht Rating Training Record Book please read the UK government briefing at:
https://www.gov.uk/government/uploads/system/uploads/attachment_data/file/327684/training_record_book_revision_22_04-2.pdf

VHF Radio

The VHF radio is an important piece of safety equipment on board. It's vitally important that the crew members responsible for it understand the correct procedures. Remember, unnecessary transmissions could block out a Mayday distress call. This course can be taken in the classroom or interactively online with a final written assessment at a test centre.

Course content includes:
- The basics of radio operation
- Correct frequencies (channels) to be used
- Distress, emergency and medical assistance procedures
- Making ship to shore telephone calls
- Search and rescue (SART)
- Emergency position indicating radio beacons (EPIRB)

Yacht Master Coastal

The Yacht Master™ Coastal will equip you with the knowledge needed to skipper a yacht on coastal cruises, no more than 60 miles from harbour, but it does not necessarily have the experience needed to undertake longer passages.

The candidate will be expected to demonstrate an understanding of all aspects of the syllabus, though they may not have had the opportunity to carry them out in practice under a range of different weather conditions.

There are some pre-requisites; all candidates must be at least seventeen years old, hold a RYA VHF Short Range Certificate or higher, and hold a valid first aid certificate dated within three years of the exam. Candidates must also have completed at least thirty days at sea, two of which should be as Skipper, and logged 800 sea miles and twelve night hours. Half the qualifying sea time must be in tidal waters.

Please check with the RYA for qualifying vessel length.

Yachtmaster Offshore

The Yachtmaster™ Offshore qualification is needed to skipper a cruising yacht on any passage during which the yacht is no more than 150 miles from harbour.

The Yachtmaster™ Offshore practical exams can be taken under sail or power and your certificate will be endorsed accordingly. The candidate or the training centre they are using provides the boat, and the RYA provides an examiner.

Prerequisites for this qualification are fifty days at sea, 2500 miles at sea (half of which must be tidal), five passages over sixty miles (including two as skipper and two overnight), the RYA Yachtmaster Offshore Theory training, RYA Yachtmaster Practical (COC) training, VHF training and a valid first aid certificate (basic STCW is acceptable). For commercial endorsement, candidates must also have one-day sea survival and a valid ENG 1.

Please check with the RYA for qualifying vessel length.

What is commercial endorsement?

Commercial endorsement is required for work on board British flagged vessels subject to the MCA's codes of practice for small commercial vessels.

Training courses for the engineering department

AEC (Approved Engine Course)

This is a five-day course designed to improve understanding of diesel engines, fuel systems, cooling systems, engine electrical systems, and more.

In order to complete this course, you must have at least one month of yacht service in the engine room.

Advanced Engineering Tickets

As you progress with your engineering career, gaining more sea time and experience you can then start to work your way through your courses to gain your tickets (qualifications). The size of the vessel you are working on will determine which ticket you must hold as a chief engineer, 2nd engineer, or 3rd engineer.

Training for the interior department

Introductory steward/ess courses

At the time of writing, it isn't a requirement for interior crew members to undertake training. However, if you *have* completed any courses to enhance your knowledge and hospitality skills, it will show potential employers that you mean business.

There are a variety of courses available for interior staff, which varies from school to school. These non-mandatory courses can give a good insight into the fundamental requirements of your role as a steward/ess and are likely to give you more confidence when you step on board for the first time.

Many training schools offer a five-day course that covers both the theory and practical aspects of basic seamanship along with training in interior duties.

Course content includes:
- How to make a bed
- Silver service
- Etiquette
- Table settings
- Ironing techniques
- Stain removal
- Flower arranging
- Cleaning methods

GUEST training program

The Professional Yacht Association (PYA) has introduced the GUEST training program in order to implement training and career progression in the interior department.

Though every other yachting department has a clear training/career progression structure in place, the interior, until recently, did not. There is even now a training record book available to log all of your experience and training. Please see the training record book section later in this chapter for more information.

Entry Level (Junior Steward/ess):

The pre-requisites and service requirements are:
- Valid ENG 1 medical certificate
- Basic STCW certificate
- No previous yacht service required
- PYA Yacht Interior Introduction certificate
- PYA Yacht Interior Basic Food Service certificate
- PYA Wine and Cocktail certificate
- Food hygiene certification

Wine and Spirit Education Trust (WSET)

Some maritime schools run Wine and Spirit Education Trust courses, but do take a look at the WSET website for full details of what they offer (http://www.wsetglobal.com/).

This can be a great way to start your wine knowledge training as WSET courses can be done online or in the classroom.

If you're keen to start improving your wine knowledge right away, I'd recommend that you download the VI Vino app for your phone. This will tell you costs, food pairings, and rankings of wines from all around the world. You can even put notes on there to remember your favourites!

Training for the galley department

Fancy your hand at cooking? Think you might be the next Gordon Ramsey or Raymond Blanc? Joining the galley team on a yacht could be a great career move for you.

Most yachts will want to employ galley staff that already has experience cooking. If you don't have this and haven't done any previous culinary training, I would highly recommend obtaining some training before you apply.

Where you go for training will depend on where you are located. There are marine cookery schools all over the world. You could also look into getting a more widely recognised training qualification such as a City and Guilds, in case you ever want to take your culinary skills back to land.

Ships' Cook Certificate

The Ships Cooks Certificate is required on all MLC compliant commercial yachts with ten or more crew members since August 2014 (unless exemption has been given by Flag).

This certificate sets out the minimum training requirements for all cooks and catering staff. It takes the form of an assessment that proves that the candidate can cook correctly and safely, including demonstration of a specific range of techniques. It's based on the City and Guilds Level 2 Professional Diploma in Cookery as issued in England and Northern Ireland.

If you have an equivalent certificate issued by an EU member State, or another administration, it will be accepted by the MLC. In addition to the equivalent SCC, the candidate must also hold a Basic STCW training certificate, a food safety or food hygiene certificate, and a valid ENG 1 Medical.

How do you qualify for the Ship's Cook Certificate (SCC)?

For shore-based cooking backgrounds with no formal qualifications:
- Twelve months working in a shore based catering establishment
- Completed assessment in marine cookery
- A food safety or food hygiene certificate
- One month of sea service, as proved by discharge book entries
- Full Basic STCW certificate
- A valid ENG 1 Medical

For shore-based cooking backgrounds with formal qualifications (Level 2 diploma standard):
- Completed assessment in marine cookery
- A food safety or food hygiene certificate
- One month of sea service, as proved by discharge book entries

- Full Basic STCW certificate
- A valid ENG 1 Medical

Please note: the option below includes those already working as a chef on board who don't yet have the SCC. If you haven't taken it yet you will need to do so ASAP.

For marine cooking backgrounds with or without formal qualifications:
- Completed assessment in marine cookery
- A food safety or food hygiene certificate
- One month of sea service, as proved by discharge book entries
- Full Basic STCW certificate
- A valid ENG 1 Medical

Galley Foundation Course

This is a five-day intensive course designed to prepare you for galley life. There are no pre-requisites, so it's ideal for those aspiring to work in the industry.

Course content includes:
- Time management
- Menu planning
- Provisioning
- Safe storage of food items
- Working while underway
- Dietary requirements

Other course options

There are many other specific galley training courses, but I would highly recommend getting an internationally recognised chef training qualification instead. This will be more versatile as it will be recognised by employers both in yachting and in other industries. You may not want to work on yachts forever!

What do you need to know about training record books?

Most yachting career paths have an official training record book that you can apply for. This is an important document as it will be where much of your training and experience is logged.

Though it may seem tedious to keep your record book up to date, you'll appreciate the effort in completing it when applying for senior level training.

Training record books for deck crew members

When you start work on deck, it is imperative that you log your sea time from the offset. How much sea time you have logged will affect which training courses and certificates you will be eligible for, and therefore whether or not you can apply for promotions.

The most effective way of logging your experience is by keeping records of your sea service in a discharge book.

There is no one definitive record book that all deck team members' use. Instead, there is a range of accepted methods to choose from:

- Merchant Navy Discharge Book (Seaman's Book)
- Certificates of Discharge from ship
- Professional Yachtsmen's Service Record Book

- MCA approved Seaman's Discharge Book: https://www.gov.uk/government/uploads/system/uploads/attachment_data/file/429001/MSF_4509_Rev_03.15_DB_BSC_Application_Form.pdf
- Nautilus Training record book: https://www.nautilusint.org/en/contact-us/
- UK Government Training Record Book (valid if most of your experience is on a vessel under 24m): **https://www.gov.uk/government/uploads/system/uploads/attachment_data/file/327684/training_record_book_revision_22_04-2.pdf**

Whichever record book system you use, the evidence you record in it will need to be supported by sea service testimonials that can be signed off by your captain or management company.

Training record books for engineer crew members

If you work on a vessel that is over 24m, you will need to log all your engineering time. Proof of this sea time can be documented using one of the following methods:

- Merchant Navy Discharge Book (Seaman's Book)
- Certificates of Discharge from ship
- Professional Yachtsmen's Service Record Book: http://www.pya.org/services

- MCA approved Seaman's Discharge Book: https://www.gov.uk/government/uploads/system/uploads/attachment_data/file/429001/MSF_4509_Rev_03.15_DB_BSC_Application_Form.pdf

Whichever record book system you use, the evidence you record in it will need to be supported by sea service testimonials that can be signed off by your captain or management company.

These records are particularly important for engineers, as they will be needed in order to be eligible for MCA courses. When it comes time to enrol in your first course, you'll need to apply to the MCA for a Letter of Initial Assessment. This Letter will provide you with the training, education, and sea service that will be required to attain you first Certificate of Competency (CoC).

You can apply for this letter using the application form found on the UK government website:

https://www.gov.uk/government/uploads/system/uploads/attachment_data/file/330599/LIA_App_Form_All_Rev_0713.pdf

Training record books for interior crew members

The PYA has recently introduced the Interior Training Record Book (ITRB). Although some of it may seem obvious when completing it, the record book is very useful for noting down experience and will help further your career in the future. Use it to monitor your progress and consider it a reflection of your performance and learning on board.

You will need to become a member of the PYA to get your own record book. Once you've completed your registration, you'll be able to download a copy of the book from:
http://www.pya.org/article/Interior-Training-Record-Book

What else do you need to know about training record books?

You will not be required to apply for a new record book each time you change to a different flagged yacht, even if you are moving from one shipping registry to another. So long as the book you have has been issued by another flag state and the information relating to your sea service is available in English, it will normally be accepted by your new employers.

The main purpose of a training record book is to record sea time. However, they do have other uses! They can help with visa applications, allow crew to fly on marine fare tickets which are often discounted and fully refundable, and have a larger luggage allowance.

The application for a British Seaman's discharge book can be found at:
https://www.gov.uk/government/uploads/system/uploads/attachment_data/file/429001/MSF_4509_Rev__03.15_DB_BSC_Application_Form.pdf

Michael's Seafarer Story

Michael is a 32-year-old Scotsman who joined yachting after extensive experience in hospitality. He initially worked as a steward before transferring to the deck team. He is now a deckhand/mate.

I found my first job through a crew agency. I did try dock walking but very quickly realised that it was not the way to find an interior position as a man. As dock walking wasn't successful for me, I wasn't able to find any day work.

During my job hunt, I stayed in a couple different types of accommodation. All the local crew houses were full when I arrived, so I checked into a budget hotel instead. I later shared an apartment with people I met while doing my STCW training, then finally moved to a caravan park for the last few weeks before I moved onto my first yacht.

Though male stewards are far from unheard of, they're not the norm. I also didn't have any previous sea experience, though I had worked for many years in high-end hotels. Because of this, I really got a mixture of reactions from both agents and experienced crew members. Some were impressed with my hospitality and boutique hotel background, but others got hung up on the fact that I had not worked in yachting before. I even had one captain trying to shoot me down on a night out, but fortunately, I managed to impress him by telling him more about my hotel experience. Many people hear 'hotel' and think of the Holiday Inn. I had actually worked with far higher profile guests than many yachting industry professionals expected.

Once I got a job on a yacht, the only thing that shocked me was how easy it was! For months everyone had been saying that I couldn't possibly imagine how demanding the job would be. As it was, I went from managing a thirty- five bedroom hotel with two rosette restaurants, a cocktail bar and a banqueting suite for a hundred guests, to working on a yacht and only dealing with a maximum of twelve guests and only working eight - ten-hour shifts.

Although I will say that now on I'm on a smaller vessel, I tend to do sixteen to twenty- two-hour shifts. If you've got previous hospitality experience, yacht work may not be as completely alien to you as people will suggest.

Chapter Seven

What to do before you travel

In order to be effectively prepared for your new career in yachting, I'd suggest you do the following *before* you travel from your home country.

Pack lightly

Crew cabins are small, which means space will be at a serious premium. Because of this, you need to travel light! It's recommended that you take a soft holdall or bag that can easily be folded or packed away. Most boats do not have room on board to store hard suitcases, so make sure not to take one.

Once you get on board you will be provided with a crew uniform and normally all necessary toiletries. All you need to take with you is your swimwear, sleepwear, clothes for interviews, day work/dock walking, and a few outfits for your leisure time.

If you don't already have a laptop, I would highly recommend investing in one that's small, lightweight, and easy to transport. If you're a reader, it's a good idea to take a Kindle or other eReader with you as they're much more lightweight than books, and you'll never run out of reading material!

It's also important to pack a small amount of stationary. A notebook and pen could be helpful during your job hunt!

Organise USB/Cloud Storage

A USB stick or cloud storage facility can be invaluable when you're travelling light or using a cloud storage system such as Dropbox. USB sticks are really handy as you will be able to use them even without Internet access.

Before you leave home, make sure you take the time to scan all your important documents such as your passport, driving licence, and any relevant qualification certificates. You'll also want to save a digital version of your CV and references. *Please note you must bring the original certificates with you!*

Invest in a job-hunting wardrobe

When you set out for the day to dock walk or visit crew agencies, what you wear will play a big role in the impression you make. The aim is to look like a crew member who's ready for a day's work. Ideally, this would mean for guys wearing a polo shirt, smart t-shirt, and shorts and for the ladies, a blouse or polo shirt with either shorts or a skort. You should also make sure to invest in a comfortable pair of boat shoes or flip-flops as you may be doing a lot of walking.

It's worth noting that there's a chance you may secure day work for that day while dock walking so it's sensible to pack a spare set of clothing suitable for working in, that you don't mind getting dirty.

For interviews you may want to consider something a little smarter. Ladies, I always think a blouse or shift style dress can give you more edge, and gents, a smart polo or a shirt.

Visit your doctor and optician

Before you travel anywhere, I'd recommend paying a visit to your doctor. This is in order to make sure your vaccinations are up to date (including any you may need for exotic locations you plan/hope to visit), and that you have a large enough stock of any prescription medication you take to last you for a minimum of six months.

If you wear glasses, you will also want to visit your optician before you leave. A second pair of glasses would be a very wise investment, and if you wear contacts, you'll need to make sure you have enough to last you for a long period away from home.

Organise your finances

There are two reasons to visit your bank before you set off to start your yachting career. First, it's a very good idea to notify your bank that you will be working overseas and will be using your debit card in other countries. This will mean they can put a note on your account that your card will be used overseas and will make it far less likely that they would consider this suspicious and put a block on your card.

Secondly, it's also worth considering which account you would like your yachting salary to be paid into. Most salaries will be paid in Euros or USD, so it's a good idea to look into getting a multi-currency bank account set up. Your existing bank may be able to offer a solution, or you could consider offshore banking options.

Set your mobile phone up for international use

You will probably want to be able to use your mobile phone while overseas. This can be the easiest way to get in touch with friends and family and will enable potential employers to get hold of you at very short notice.

Using your phone without any preparations will likely result in a very large bill! Avoid this by considering one of the following options:
- Unlock your phone so you will be able to pick up and use a local SIM card when you arrive at your destination;
- Get a roaming SIM card if you think you may be travelling between countries;
- Contact your current mobile phone provider to see if they offer competitive rates on international calling packages;
- Look into so-called 'feel at home' packages from Three Mobile (and others) for good rates on local calls from your chosen yachting hub.

Get your taxes in order

If you are leaving the UK, you will need to inform HMRC. They will ask you to complete a P85 form, which advises them that you are leaving the country. It will also save you time in the future if you ask them to allocate you a seafarer's tax code before you leave.

HMRC can be quite helpful if you give them a call, although be warned that you may wait on the line a while!

If you are in the UK the phone number is: 0300 200 3300.
From abroad it is: +441355359022.

Getting this in order before you travel will save a lot of problems later on. As an added bonus, if you're leaving before year's end and have been working for the entire tax year, you could be entitled to a little rebate.

More information about this is available on the UK Government website at: https://www.gov.uk/government/publications/income-tax-leaving-the-uk-getting-your-tax-right-p85 and https://www.gov.uk/government/publications/seafarers-earnings-deduction-hs205-self-assessment-helpsheet.

If travelling from other countries, it is best to check with your local tax authority to find out the right course of action prior to your departure.

Ensure your passport is up to date

This one may sound obvious, but you'd be surprised how many people fail to check their passport! In order to travel to many international destinations, you will need to ensure that you have more than six months left on your passport.

I'd also recommend that you scan your passport, leave a copy with your next of kin and save a copy to a cloud storage facility. This will be really helpful if you ever lose it.

Visa research

It's really important to do your research on visa requirements *before* you leave home. Visas can be a bit of a grey area when you're working in the yachting industry, so make sure you check and double-check that your paperwork is in order.

Relevant visas may be:

- *Schengen Visa*

    The Schengen is for non-EU residents who are travelling to the EU. It will allow you to freely travel within the twenty-five Schengen territories of the EU, including the entire Western Med.

    To see if your country of citizenship requires the Schengen visa visit: http://en.wikipedia.org/wiki/Schengen_Area

When your Schengen visa expires, you will need to travel to a non-Schengen state to renew it. Please double-check this information first, laws change and this is merely a guide. The responsibility lies with you.

- <u>*B1 visa*</u>

    B1 visas allow non-US and non-Canadian citizens to work on a foreign flagged vessel in American waters. You must apply for this visa at a US Embassy/Consulate *before* traveling to the USA.

PLEASE NOTE: You will normally have to show a contract of employment and a copy of the ship's papers before a visa of this sort will get issued. I would advise <u>against</u> applying for this visa off your own back and rather waiting until you have a contract of employment or the vessel you are joining is heading there. They should be happy to arrange this paperwork for you.

If you are not a US citizen, you cannot work on a US boat unless you have a Green Card or some form of US residency. A B1/B2 visa will not be sufficient.

Once you have made an appointment at the US embassy, you must be sure you have the proper documentation. This will include:
- Completed visa application
- Anti-terrorism checklist
- Proof of a residence in your home country

- Proof of strong ties to your home country to show you do not intend to abandon it

Need to know more about the B1/B2 visa? Further information can be found on the following websites:
- www.embassyinformation.com
- http://travel.state.gov/visa/temp/types/types_1262.html
- http://www.workpermit.com/us/employer_b1_b2.htm

Apply for a Seaman's Discharge book

A Seaman's Book is a record of a seaman's career certifications and experiences. You can apply for a Seaman's Discharge book through various maritime authorities.

To apply you will need:
- A letter of employment
- A copy of the certificate of registry
- The fee: usually around £40 by post or £90 by personal appointment

The British Seaman's Discharge Book is the official MCA and Red Ensign Group logbook, for which any British citizen (or any non-British citizen employed on a UK-flagged vessel) can apply. Find application details here: https://www.gov.uk/government/publications/application-for-a-discharge-book-andor-british-seamans-card-msf-4509   or https://www.gov.uk/get-seamans-discharge-book-or-british-seamans-card.

The MCA also accepts other approved service record books, such as the Professional Yachtsmen's Association (PYA) Service Record Book.

Whichever option you go for, a seaman's book is absolutely essential for crew who do not form part of the EU. This is because they allow for crew to fly on marine airfare tickets, which are often heavily discounted, fully refundable, fully changeable, and come with additional luggage allowance.

Decide when to travel

Certain times of year are better than others for joining the yachting industry. Generally, you will want to travel out in time for the beginning of the season. The season in the Mediterranean generally runs from April/May until the end of September/early October. The US/Caribbean season commences around November and runs to around March/April.

If you have a limited budget to last you while on the job hunt then the trick is to not be too early and to not leave it too late.

The best tactic is to try to position yourself in one of the main hubs at the start of the new season, just as the boats will be getting crewed up.

Decide where to travel

There are yachting hubs all over the world. Which one you go to will depend largely on practicalities and personal preference. As a general rule, it tends to be much easier for most worldwide crew to start off in the Med instead of the USA due to visa restrictions.

Here's a quick taster of your choices:

- ***The Mediterranean***

    Antibes in the South of France has historically been the main yachting hub in Europe. Today it is still the hub most visited by new crew due to its easily accessible ports and shipyards, easy access to the coast of Italy via train, and the vast number of crew agencies that are based there.

    Palma is also a popular hangout for crew looking for work. It has a more relaxed and chilled-out vibe than Antibes and is very popular with sailing yacht crew. There are a much smaller pool of crew agencies based in Palma and the ports tend to be more difficult to access as they're not open like they are in Antibes and a lot of the Cote d'Azur.

    Barcelona has recently become *the* new place to attract crew. This is mainly due to the new Marina Port Vell and the growing popularity of MB92 shipyard. Other attractions may include cheaper accommodation and living expenses and a varied nightlife.

- *Fort Lauderdale*

When the US/Caribbean season kicks off, crew seem to flock like birds to Fort Lauderdale. This is a major yachting hub with crew agencies and crew housing all over town. However, you *have* to have the right visa to commence your search there. I wouldn't necessarily recommend starting your job-hunt over there unless you are a seasoned yachtie and already know the drill.

- *Caribbean – St Marteen/Antigua*

Due to the visa restrictions on entering the USA, more and more crew are heading to the Caribbean Islands of St Marteen and Antigua to conduct their search for work.

The busy period here is between December and February and some crew agents open pop-up offices for a few months during this time. Local shore support agencies can also be a good resource for crew.

Olivia's Seafarer Story

Olivia is a chef who joined the yachting industry in 2004. She no longer works on board but moved into land-based chef positions in Monaco and London with the same type of clientele. Here is a day in her life story as a sole chef for eighteen crew members on a yacht delivery to the Pacific.

I woke up at 7am, got ready for the day, and started work at 7.30am. My first task was to make a smoothie for the crew, followed by breakfast prep. As we were at sea, many of the crew had been up all night and needed a hearty breakfast. This was served at 9am, and then I started to prep for lunch.

I liked to give the crew healthy, nutritious food. It was so important to keep everyone well nourished, especially when you are working long hours in a physically demanding role. This was sometimes a challenge, especially at the end of a crossing with limited fresh produce left. I generally provided five dishes for the crew: a soup, protein, a carb dish, and two veggie/salad options.

Once lunch was done, it was time to clean up, then to have a break and eat something myself. At sea, I loved sitting out on deck surrounded by the ocean.

Most of my afternoon was spent preparing dinner, which would be served to the crew at 6pm. This was followed by a big clean-up that included ensuring all fridges were clean and organised. My final task was to write a menu for the next day before finishing up at around 7.30pm.

Of course, this was a day on a crossing where I was just cooking for the crew. If we were mid-charter and there were guests on board, there would be so much more work to do! It would mean starting earlier, perhaps even 5.30 am, and finishing at around 10 or 11pm, or maybe even later, especially if guests wanted snacks in the middle of the night!

It can be a very hard job, but I have so many amazing memories, many from my time in the Pacific as it's just paradise. It has amazing sea life, diving, paradise beaches, black pearls, surf competitions, Tahitian dancing, and delicious food like Poisson Cru. My dream was to see the Pacific, and it lived up to my expectations and more.

Chapter Eight

The Job Hunt

There are many ways to search for work in the yachting industry. You can contact recruitment agencies, join yachting Facebook groups where jobs are advertised, read local yachting publications, and leave your CV or business card on noticeboards, dock walk or network.

Please feel free to join our group; we would love for you to be part of our community. This can be helpful either while you are job hunting in a yachting hub or if you're looking for advice or a travel companion before you go. Please do feel free to ask questions. You can join at: https://www.facebook.com/groups/YachtingIndustryUK/

Will I be able to find work from my home country?

There are always exceptions, and this does happen, but if you are new to yachting, it's not normally possible to secure your first position from home.

Employers and agents alike will want to meet newcomers face-to-face. Because of this, it's important that you base yourself in one of the yachting hubs so you're available for interviews. In most cases, interviews are offered on very short notice (sometimes the same day), so arranging them from home in advance is not normally an option.

Yachting positions tend to be filled very quickly, so if you want the best chance of getting a job, you'll need to be ready and waiting where the action is!

What do you need to know about applying for your first position?

When a position is advertised, please make sure that you **only** apply for it if you meet *all* of the requirements of the job. For example, if the yacht is looking for a minimum of six months experience this actually means they will *only* consider candidates who have this experience.

In other industries, you may be able to charm your way into a role you're not quite qualified for, but this is not normally the case in yachting.

Not only will applying anyway highlight that you are under-qualified, it will also indicate to any potential employers or crew agents that you are unable to follow instructions. Understanding and accepting this right away will save both you and other people a lot of wasted time!

It can be very difficult and frustrating when trying to secure your very first position in yachting, but if you are prepared, have the right attitude and remain enthusiastic, it will happen!

How long will it take to find a job?

This is not a question with a straightforward answer. You could be super lucky and land a yachting job in a day, but it could take weeks or even months.

Please do not be under the illusion that this will be easy. The competition is fierce, and there will be a lot of applicants for each role. Some job hunters do get lucky and find themselves in the right place at the right time, but in most cases, whether or not you get a job will depend on you, the effort made with writing your CV, your appearance, and most importantly, your personality.

In other words, the only way to ensure success is to motivate yourself and get out there, day after day, dock walking, networking and talk to as many industry people as you can, and make sure you make a positive impression on them. There are hundreds of other potential crew members that all want the same job as you, so why should you be the one to get hired? Think about it, and make sure you have the answer to that question!

The hardest job to get in yachting will be your first one. The best advice I can give you is to be the best applicant you can, create a good image, take the appropriate training courses, get a good quality CV, network as much as possible, and be well presented at all times.

What are employers looking for?

In short, employers are looking for enthusiastic individuals who know how to conduct themselves in all situations. The best job candidates are polite, are able to follow instructions, are forward thinking, are well-groomed, and simply *ooze* enthusiasm.

When you set out to dock walk or visit crew agencies, make sure you:
- Are well turned out

- Are not hungover
- Do not smell of smoke or alcohol
- Are clean shaven/neatly made up
- Have neat and tidy hair
- Are wearing smart, ironed clothes
- Are friendly but professional
- Have plenty of business cards and a well-presented CV

Once you're looking for your second or third job, potential employers will start to look at how long you have stuck with each position. Unless you're doing day work (more on that later), employers will be looking for longevity and proof of your commitment and loyalty to your previous employers. A busy CV where you have literally jumped from boat to boat will raise concerns.

What employers are NOT looking for?

It is so important to keep your reputation intact. Crew renowned for drinking, fighting, drugs, breaching vessel security, and/or stealing will struggle to get hired. Yachting is a very close-knit industry, and you should be aware that word gets around fast. When you are out in a bar, keep in mind that your future captain could very well be standing behind you.

Writing an effective CV

Creating an effective yachting CV is an extremely important aspect of your job hunt. Do remember that this will be your first contact with potential employers and that you need to create a lasting, positive impression.

Your CV is a tool used to sell yourself as a professional and qualified candidate.

Hopefully, you don't need me to tell you that all the information on your CV should be accurate, up to date, and most importantly, TRUE. You should also aim for it to give an insight into your character and relay the message to a crew agent or captain that you would be an asset to the boat.

A bad CV can stop even extremely qualified people from getting a job. If you feel you have strong transferable skills, look the part, have all your training bases covered *and* have a killer personality but are still not getting invited to interviews, then your CV is almost definitely the problem.

There is help available should you find it difficult to write your CV. Professionals such as The Career Concierge (**www.career-concierge.com**) are on hand to support you through the writing process. Though there is a cost involved, it will be a very small investment if it helps you to jumpstart your career.

On a practical note, please do make sure to double-check the size of your CV (plus accompanying photo) before you send it. Most crew agents will request CVs of under 2MB. There is a reason for this. Many yachts have variable Internet speeds and may not be able to open or download larger files. If your CV is too large and proves difficult to open, it's highly likely that it will get discarded.

Take a look at the sample to get an idea of layout!

Sample CV

Your Name – Desired Position at the top

Phone number:	Include the country codes
Email Address:	Make this a professional email
Skype:	
Nationality:	
DOB:	Please write the month 20 July 1980
Languages Spoken:	English mother tongue, French advanced
Health: Smoker, visible tattoos	
Visas:	B1/B2 expires 2018
Current Location:	French Riviera
Availability:	1 week

Insert your photograph here

This should be a head and shoulder photo, wearing yachting attire, such as polo shirt, shirt or blouse.

Photo to be taken with either a plain background or in a yachting relevant location.

No sunglasses including resting on the head, no heavy make-up or jewellery to be worn.

Profile/Objectives

Introduce yourself and sell yourself. Here is where you write a brief sales pitch about you.

Add what position you are seeking, if you are looking for a private or charter vessel, and the size range. Please be very specific here, but equally, do NOT limit yourself. If you are open to private or charter, then make sure you detail this.

If you are ONLY looking for a job on the French Riviera, then please state this so that someone who is hiring for a world cruising vessel doesn't waste their time on contacting you, or alternatively if you are free and open to travel make this very clear.

Qualifications

- STCW Basic Safety Training
- Proficiency in Security Awareness
- PBL2
- BA Hons

Employment History

Start with your most recent position and work your way backwards.

Month 2012 – Month 2014   44m MY BOAT   Deckhand

I worked on board MY XXX for 8 months in the position of XXX. It was a busy private/charter yacht that ran a dual season program in both the Med and Caribbean.

During my time with this vessel, I completed two Atlantic crossings. My duties included...

Keep your job descriptions uniform, detail each position in date order, and keep the format the same. Employers like to read a CV that is clearly laid out and pleasing to the eye.

REMEMBER attention to detail is extremely important.

Your most recent positions should have the most detail, as these are more relevant to a potential employer.

Make sure to detail the experiences you have had in each position by giving a truthful insight to your skill set and knowledge

Hobbies & Interests

List what you enjoy doing in your spare time. Do you play rugby, dive, go running, sew, cook as a hobby, and/or enjoy reading? This is a good way to gain a little insight as to what you like to do in your downtime. When placing crew, it is helpful to pair crew who enjoy similar recreational activities. If you are a party animal who enjoys late nights, would you be happy working on a teetotal boat with a bunch of fitness fanatics who are in their beds by 930pm each night?

This is also a chance to add other information, such as you are currently training for your pilot's license or have a long-term goal to become a yoga teacher. Or maybe you enjoy learning about wines and have plans for your next break to do a wine and spirits course.

References

References are so important. Be sure to put the most recent reference first and work your way backwards. Make sure you have permission from your reference for agents and potential employers to contact them.

Also, if you have not been in contact with your reference for a year or more, contact them to advise that you are looking for work again, to find out if you may use them. Also, make sure that they are still at the contact number and email you have listed. REMEMBER they may have moved on too!

M/Y NAME OF BOAT
Captain name
+33 123 456 789
mate@gmail.com

M/Y NAME OF BOAT
Chief Stewardess name
+1 954 123 456 78
Chstew@hotmail.com

M/Y NAME OF BOAT

Chief Mate name

+39 123 456 789

mate@googlemail.com

Hints:

- Make sure you keep your font the same.
- Also, make sure that you only use 2 to 3 sizes.
- Keep your text paragraphs JUSTIFIED, as this keeps it looking neat and tidy.
- Read and re-read your CV to check it for spelling, typing errors, and grammatical errors.
- Considering hiring a professional yachting CV writer who can help you with this.

Choosing a photograph

It is standard practice for CVs in the yachting industry to include a photograph. This should be a formal head and shoulder image of you that you've had taken specially. Please don't just attach your current Facebook profile picture.

Ideally, your photograph should be taken outside in natural light, as these are generally the most flattering images. Some vessels will ask for a full-length photograph, so it's always worth having some taken so you have them if requested.

Professional attire is non-negotiable for your photograph. This means a shirt or blouse plus smart trousers, shorts, or skirt. (I would usually recommend that women wear a skirt for full-length shots). If you are a chef, I would highly recommend having your photo taken wearing your chef whites.

Things not to do: avoid wearing your sunglasses, a hat or any noticeable jewellery. Over-the-top makeup or complicated hairstyles are also a bad idea. You're aiming to present yourself as a professional.

Finally, your photo should be a positive reflection of you. Please don't be afraid to smile!

How to get the best from crew agents

Crew agents are recruitment agencies that specifically cater for the yachting industry. They are located all over the world, but you will find lots of them in each of the yachting hubs, and more and more online.

Yachts will approach a crew agent with details of the roles they need to fill and a set of guidelines about what kind of people they are looking for. Agents will interview, vet, and reference check potential candidates as well as handling practicalities such as the candidate's availability and location.
It is extremely worthwhile to build strong professional relationships with crew agents. They can be an excellent resource both during your first job hunt and later on when you are looking to advance your career.

Most agencies will require you to complete an online registration. It will save time if you do this before you even leave home. No matter how thoroughly you've completed this registration, as soon as you arrive in the hub *you need to go and introduce yourself to the crew agents in person.*

Remember to:
- Let them know that you are in town, you are available now, and what position you are looking for;
- Be polite and presentable;
- Ensure your online profiles have the correct location and contact details;
- Make sure you have given full details of your experience and qualifications.

<u>Please note</u> that you should *never* have to pay an agency to join. This is illegal, and if you're ever asked to part with cash to try and obtain a job, please stay well away! Crew agents make their money by being paid a finder's fee by the yacht once a crew member has been placed on board, not from job hunters themselves.

<u>*What happens once you've registered?*</u>

There will be a lot of other hopefuls out there looking for work at exactly the same time as you are. Unfortunately, it's very unlikely that there will be enough jobs for all the people looking. Signing up with a handful of recruitment agencies is no guarantee that they will be able to find you a job.

You can maximise your chances by ensuring you can always be contacted by phone and that you are ready to take on day work or go for an interview at extremely short notice. It's not uncommon for job hunters to be offered day work at 7.30am to start at 8am. Make sure you are ready by *always* keeping your phone on and audible, and by treating every morning as a work day: get up, get dressed, and be ready to leave at very short notice.

<u>Stay on the good side of your recruitment agents</u>

It pays to remember that crew agents are as keen to impress senior yachting crew as you are. After all, it's the yachts that pay their fees.

Because of this, agents will only want to recommend the very best candidates for each position that's available. Typically they'll only send a handful of the highest quality CVs that match the exact criteria of the position to the boat. It's inadvisable for job hunters to question this process or to try and persuade a recruitment agent to put them forward for a job for which they are not qualified or experienced to do.

If you are lucky enough to be offered day work or an interview, please remember that your behaviour while on the boat will reflect both on yourself *and* on the crew agent that recommended you. Turning up late or not presenting yourself well will make both you and your agent look bad.

What happens after an interview?

After you attend an interview organised by a crew agent, you will be expected to call, email or visit the agent afterwards for feedback. They will want to know how it went, and whether you are interested in accepting the job should they make you an offer.

If and when you do get hired, the agent who helped you get there will want to know your start date and agreed salary. It is also good manners to update your online profiles with all the other agencies with which you have registered to let them know you are no longer looking for work. This will enable them to update their records and ensure they are only keeping open files on active job hunters.

What's the deal with dock walking?

Dock walking is a very common way for hopeful yachting crew to get work. Basically, it's exactly as it sounds: you walk the docks to look for a job.

To get started, walk up and down the docks in any given port and speak to each boat to find out if they are looking for day workers or full-time crew. I know this can sound intimidating, but do bear in mind that everyone has to start somewhere. Most of the crew you'll speak to will have dock walked themselves at some point in their career.

Want to get it right? Here are some tips for success:

Pick your time carefully

Typically the best time of day to walk the docks is in the short window between 7.30am and 8.30am when crew are likely to need staff for that day. You could also try at the end of the working day between 3.30pm - 5.00pm, as vessels may be looking for extra help for the following day.

Be smartly dressed
Presentation is hugely important when dock walking as the yacht crew you speak to will have to make a very quick judgment on whether or not you are what they're looking for. Either wear smart work-appropriate clothing or make sure you're carrying spare shorts and a polo shirt in case you're offered day work on the spot. Not all day workers get a uniform provided.

Prepare for success
When you're dock walking, you should ensure you have plenty of business cards and CVs ready to hand out to any interested boats. It goes without saying that these should all be up to date and have the correct contact details.

Be mindful about which vessels you approach
It's not a good idea to approach any vessels that appear to be in guest mode. If you see flowers on the aft, the furniture is uncovered, the cushions are out, and/or the crew are wearing more formal attire, do not try and draw their attention to ask for work. Leave that boat and approach it at another time when they no longer have guests on.

Take a notebook with you

It's sensible to keep track of which boats you have already approached.

Dockwalk alone

It is so much better for you if you walk the docks alone to look for work. You will look more confident. Remember that if you walk in a pair or a group, you will be competing for the same jobs.

Don't take rejection personally

If you're approaching yachts unsolicited, you need to accept that rejection is a natural part of the process. Many yachts will be fully crewed and just won't need the extra help. Try not to get discouraged. Perseverance and remaining positive will go a long way during your job hunt. Plus if they know of a vessel looking for extra help they may point you in the right direction.

How important is networking?

In this industry, who you know is vital. As you will soon learn, the yachting industry is a small, connected world where word travels very quickly! Because of this, it's important to get out there and make a *good* name for yourself. (Note the emphasis on *good*).

I've had personal experience of how interconnected the industry is in a number of ways. More than once, I've overheard people ahead of me at the bar mention my name and others in my network. I've also often been made aware of what's being said about me, and my colleagues through the grapevine. The point it to just remember that everyone is connected somehow.

There's an industry saying that you should always act as if your future captain is standing behind you. To be honest, in any given yachting hub, they really might be. Keep this in mind when you're conducting yourself around town, whether it is a networking event, yachtie bar, a supermarket, or at the beach... you just never know.

Networking can happen at organised events, but it can also happen organically in your everyday activities. Make friends with your flat mates, roommates, and neighbours. You never know when someone will get a call for day work, be unavailable, and recommend you instead. It also pays to be open to conversation when you're out and about. A lot of people around yachting hubs will have valuable contacts or may even be responsible for hiring and firing themselves. Don't be afraid to offer a CV or business card to anyone you think might help.

Got an interview? Great. It's another networking opportunity. Even if the job itself doesn't look like it's going to work out, leave a business card anyway and ask your interviewer to please pass on your details if they hear of a role that would more suit you. The other great thing about interviews is they can get you inside ports with security guards that aren't usually open to the public. If this happens, make sure you stay inside once the interview is over and use the opportunity to dock walk.

Finally, please remember that networking should be a sober affair. It's not advisable to go out partying every night while you're job hunting. For one thing, word travels fast. For another, you should be first on the dock the next morning, bright-eyed and bushy-tailed.

Should you day work?

It is really good to try and obtain day work when starting out in the yachting industry. This is when you are offered short-term work on board that's only guaranteed on a day-to-day basis. Yachts generally take on day workers during periods when they are in port or the shipyard.

The downside of day work is that it comes with no guarantee of longer-term work. You could find yourself spending a whole season doing day work on a variety of boats without gaining a full-time position. Although this can be unsettling to not have a more secure, steadier form of income, this can actually turn out quite well in the long run.

Any time you spend day working, is time that you will be networking with crew. It's also the easiest and quickest way to gain experience working on different sizes and builds of boats. By the end of your time as a day worker, your network will have grown so much that if you are a good worker with a good reputation, your day working supervisors will recommend you if they hear of any positions coming up.

Keep this in mind and always think of day work as an all-day interview. Be sure to do a great job, work hard, and maintain a positive attitude at all times. Carry out any duties you are given, be polite, ooze enthusiasm for every task, have a can-do attitude, and offer to assist in other areas such as unloading shopping and cleaning up after meal times. Even if the yacht you are on does not have permanent work for you, they may know someone who's looking. A lot of this industry works on word of mouth so make sure you keep your reputation intact.

Where can you stay while you're looking for work?

One of the great things about work on a yacht is that your accommodation is included. However, you will need somewhere to stay while you're looking for a position or doing day work. This can be tricky as it's impossible to know how long it will take you to get a job.

Some job hunters check into budget hotels or apartment-share with other yachting hopefuls. But the most popular accommodation types are crew houses.

Crew houses are very much like hostels but are specifically designed for yacht crew. Rent is paid by either the week or the night, although some houses will give you a discounted rate if you pay for a full month at a time. Take advantage of these offers, but make sure you ask about reimbursement should you get a job before your month is up.

The rooms are typical dormitory style, and you'll be sharing with between two and eight people. Some houses will allocate rooms based on gender, but others will have mixed dormitories.

Other facilities vary from crew house to crew house. There will be shared bathroom and kitchen facilities, and most houses normally have a lounge area, Wi-Fi, and computer/printing facilities. The owners of the crew houses are generally very clued up on the industry and have often worked on yachts themselves. This means they're often able to offer sound advice.

While it may not feel overly appealing to stay in a crew house, it's a really good way to meet other crew members. Some will be looking for work for the first time, and others will already have experience to share.

Another bonus of staying in a crew house is that agents, yachts, and captains looking for day workers will sometimes phone to see if there is anyone available for work. Crew house managers can also be helpful contacts as they're often asked for recommendations for new hires.

Crew houses are typically very popular, and though you can sometimes just turn up, you're likely to need to book ahead or join a waiting list.

What do you need to understand about references?

References are vital in the yachting industry. They are generally taken very seriously, and it's very unlikely that a yacht would take you on without asking for them.

This advice stands even if you're new to the industry. The references you provide will still be hugely important, even though they will be from previous employers who may be completely unrelated to the industry. It's a good idea to prepare for this by obtaining written references from these previous employers that promote any transferable skills.

You don't necessarily need to have worked for someone for a long period before they can be used as a reference. If you have made some good contacts while day working, it's well worth asking them if they would be willing to write a reference or be contacted by a potential employer.

A few other things to keep in mind when it comes to references:
- Always keep the reference information on your CV up to date;
- Double-check email addresses and phone numbers for typing errors;
- Make sure you've asked permission from the references you've listed in advance. Some boats will check references *before* they offer you an interview;
- Contact your references each time you recommence your job hunt to make sure they're still happy to vouch for you and that their contact details haven't changed

What else do you need to keep in mind during the job hunt?

Getting work in the USA

Though Fort Lauderdale is a fantastic yachting hub to visit, it's not always an ideal place to start your job hunt for the first time if you are not a US citizen. To begin with, it's hard for non-US citizens to obtain day work.

Most international "yachties" who travel to Fort Lauderdale do so on a B1/B2 visa. This visa does not qualify you to look for temporary or day work. If you're found day working by immigration officials, you risk the loss of your B1/B2 visa and could face deportation.

I have also heard of job hunters travelling to the US on the visa waiver program to look for work. The visa waiver program is a visa for holidays only. You cannot gain employment on a holiday visa. If you enter the US and secure a position while on a tourist visa, you will then have to fly out of the US to apply for the B1 once you have your paperwork in check. The best thing to do is do your own research first. However, it's simpler to commence your yachting career in the Mediterranean.

Couples positions

Some couples set out to look for work with the intention of getting on a yacht together. Though this is a very nice idea, in practice it's unlikely to happen if you're both new to the industry.
It's not necessarily very wise to tell crew agents or potential employers that you are only looking for a job with your partner. This can be very off-putting and will seriously restrict your placement options. Even when you've spent years in the industry and have a good reputation and heaps of contacts, it can still be very hard to find a position as a couple. Don't limit your chances of employment right at the beginning by doing this.

If you're serious about your career in the industry, you will need to be prepared to accept jobs on separate boats, at least for a season or two while you gain experience and build your reputation.

Smoking, drinking, and drugs

Depending on the vessel's policies, smoking can be a deal breaker. Some boats have a strict no-smoking policy for their crew members.

If you think you can cope without smoking for a few days, a week, or potentially longer when on charter, then you might be able to make it work. But, be honest, could you really cope with being out on anchor for a few days without being able to come shore side for a cigarette? My advice is to give up smoking now. It might restrict your job opportunities, *and* it's bad for your health.

As an extra word of advice: if a crew agent asks you if you smoke, don't lie about it. If you do, you can pretty much guarantee that you'll be spotted out on a Friday night with a cigarette in hand. Yachting hubs are not huge places, and you'll likely be eating in the same restaurants and drinking in the same bars as the people you're trying to persuade to hire you.

Drinking a reasonable amount is normal and is unlikely to be looked down on. Saying that, this is a close-knit environment, and if you overdo it, you can get a bad reputation for yourself very quickly. If it's your dream to get a job on a yacht, then you may want to tone down your nights out during the job-hunting phase. There will be time for celebrations further down the line once you've proved yourself.

Finally, drugs. Like many industries, yachting has a zero tolerance policy for drug abuse. Unlike many other industries, your employers can undertake random drug testing. If you were to fail a drug test, it would result in immediate dismissal. That reputation could stick around for a long time, and it could be very difficult for you to secure a position on another vessel.

What about tattoos?

Yachting is all about presentation. Unfortunately, tattoos do not fit the image of the perfect crew member. If you have a tattoo on your hands, wrists, arms, neck, feet, leg, or anywhere else visible, then the reality is that your chances of employment could be reduced.

Many boats will specify no tattoos in their job adverts. The few that don't may be more flexible, but are likely to expect any tattoos you do have to be sufficiently covered while you're working. If you don't already have a tattoo, it might be best to wait to get inked until you after you've left the industry. If you *really* can't wait, make sure you choose a concealed area.

Email addresses

Please make sure you have a sensible email address before you start applying for jobs! Over my time in the industry, I've encountered some interesting, eyebrow-raising, and not-so-professional email addresses that *did not* make me consider the candidate as excellent yacht material!

If you want to be taken seriously, make sure you have an email that contains your first and/or last name. It takes a couple of minutes to set up a free email account online, so there really is no excuse.

This same rule applies when creating passwords for your online crew agency accounts. Be aware that most crew agents will usually be able to see what words you have chosen! Let's just say that some of the colourful language and phrases used in passwords has been quite surprising…

<u>Social Media</u>

Facebook, in particular, is a really good platform for networking, meeting other like-minded crew, searching for jobs, and finding accommodation.

Crew agents will use Facebook to connect with you as this is not only a good way for them to advertise positions, but also to check out your profile photo to see if your CV photo is a true reflection of you, and to get a feel for your lifestyle. Because of this, it's very important to be mindful of any content you've posted that will be visible to them.

I'd also like to point out that yachting hubs are often friendly places, and you're likely to actively choose to connect with the industry professionals and crew agents you meet socially. Keep these new online friends in mind whenever you post a new status or photo!

Reading yachting publications

If you want to get ahead in your career, one of the best tips I can give you is to research, research, and more research!

We may have the Internet right at our fingertips, but the more old-fashioned ways to learn about the industry are still incredibly valuable. In addition to immersing yourself with information about the industry online in forums and on websites, take a look at local yachting publications.

These will keep you informed about current happenings in the industry, including news articles, opinion pieces, and information about upcoming events. You can pick up the magazines inside crew agencies or read many of them online:

- Dockwalk   www.dockwalk.com
- Triton   www.thetriton.com
- Yachting Magazine   www.yachtingmagazine.com
- Crew Report   www.thecrewreport.com

Alfie's Seafarer Story

Alfie is from Australia and joined the yachting industry in 1999. He has been a yacht captain since 2006 and now holds a Master 3000gt ticket.

When I joined the industry in 1999, things were very different. I had no idea about yachting and stumbled into it by chance. I was backpacking my way across the Greek islands when a guy I was working with told me that his father delivered sailing yachts around the world. It sounded like a great lifestyle.

My only life plan at the time was to get to Brazil for the New Year's Eve festival because I thought it would be the best place to see in the year 2000! My colleague suggested I head to the south of France and ask around for work in exchange for a ride to the US as it would be easy to get to Brazil from there. I only had 1300 Australian dollars to my name, so it sounded like a very attractive plan!

Once the season finished in Greece, I convinced some of the other guys I was working with to come with me. We arrived in Nice, found a hostel, and checked out some of the marinas. We were blown away by the number and size of the yachts down there.

Initially, we really weren't sure what to do or if it was going to work out for us. All the yachts we looked at all appeared very professional and specialised. It took a few days, but finally, I worked up the nerve to approach someone on one of the yachts. I said something along the lines of, "Can you help me? I don't know who to speak with or what to do but I'm looking for work."

To my surprise, he gave me a list of agencies in Antibes, told me which bars I should go to, and even gave me a few numbers. His advice was to go up to every boat and every person until I got some work.

So we did that, and sure enough, after a couple of days, we got our first bit of day work getting a boat ready for the Cannes boat show. The person that gave me the job is now my oldest and best friend in the industry.

What I remember most about my early years in the industry is that everybody was very helpful. Of course, even back then there was a sort of rivalry about the size and status of the boat you worked on, where it was, and where it went.

The first time my yacht sailed into Antibes, I was unsure about what to expect because we thought it was going to be very cliquey. As it turns out, I loved it! I bought an apartment, met some of my best friends, and have been living here for nearly 10 years.

Chapter Nine
Interview tips and techniques

If you have successfully secured an interview, then well done! You will now get to meet a prospective employer either face-to-face, on the phone, or via Skype. This is your opportunity to dazzle them with your awesome personality!

The secret to a successful interview is to present yourself in a positive and confident manner without being too overbearing. Easier said than done? Don't worry. In this chapter, I've put together some key tips to help you achieve interview success.

Interview preparation

Though you won't be able to predict exactly what your interviewer will ask you, there are certain things that are very likely to come up. During your interview preparations, make sure you think about and come up with a good response to the following questions:

- What would be your ideal job scenario?

- What kind of employer and environment are you ideally looking for?

- Are you open to any size vessel and itinerary?

- How long do you plan to stay in the industry, and what career development training are you prepared to undertake?

- What are your long terms goals and objectives?

- Do you have any transferable skills or qualifications that do not pertain directly to yachting? (E.g. beauty or massage therapist, yoga instructor, personal trainer, nanny, teacher, plumber, carpenter, mechanic, fishing specialist, dive or kite surf instructor)

- Can you think of a time where you had a difficult situation with a customer or manager and how you dealt with it and resolved it?

- Can you name a time when you functioned as a part of a team and what your contribution was?

- Can you think of a time in your job where you provided successful leadership?

It's also vital to do your research. Skipping this step could mean that you put your proverbial foot in your mouth mid-interview and miss out on the opportunity.

I'd suggest you start by re-reading the job description to be sure that you are clear on the details of the position you have applied for. It's also wise to re-read your own CV so that you're prepared to go through your career history in detail, focusing on your key skills and achievements to date.

There is so much information available online that there's now very little excuse for not researching about the industry. Also, prior to your interview, if you can, try and find out details of the yacht. If there's any information you can't find online, your crew agent (if you're using one) should know.

- Where the vessel has travelled historically
- What size it is
- Who built it
- How many crew work on board
- What nationalities are represented on board

Finally, prepare any questions you have for the interviewer. These could include questions about the crew and schedule of the vessel.

What to take with you

If you're having a face-to-face interview, there will be a number of documents you'll need to take with you. If your interview is being done over the phone or Skype, you'll still need to prepare these in advance just in case you need to refer to them or send copies to your interviewer.

These documents include:

- Your CV (the interviewer may want to look at it again during the interview and may not have it to hand)
- Training certificates/qualifications
- References
- Your passport
- Any necessary visas

As a side note, please ensure that you get in touch with your references in advance to let them know that they could be contacted. If the interview is successful, they're likely to hear from your potential employers shortly afterwards. Some interviewers and most agencies do so ahead of time.

The logistics

Timekeeping is seriously important in the yachting industry. If you are late for an interview, it will have a big impact on your chances. Keep this in mind when you are planning your journey. Will you have to travel by car, bus, train or plane, or can you walk to your interview? Always plan to arrive early, that way you won't be flustered and will have a bit of flexibility should you get delayed, stuck in traffic or have your train cancelled!

You will also want to give the logistics some thought if you are expecting a phone or Skype interview. Double-check your Internet connection or phone signal, and make sure you have chosen a quiet spot where you won't be interrupted.

The A-Z of the interview

Appearance

Your appearance will not only show that you're taking the opportunity seriously, but also that you're eager to make a good impression, and that you understand that first impressions count.

- Avoid heavy makeup or over-the-top hairdos as these may distract the interviewer.
- Opt for make-up in neutral shades and neat hairstyles.
- Strong smells and heavy perfumes can offend the interviewer. If you must wear a scent, apply it lightly.
- By all means, wear sunglasses on your way to the interview, but make sure you remove them once you get there. Eye contact is vital.
- If you're a smoker, try not to smell of smoke.
- Do not chew gum.
- Men, remove any piercings, and women, limit yourself to one pair of simple earrings if you wear them.
- Make sure you have considered your hands and feet, have clean fingernails, and remember that personal care is important in this industry.

<u>*Behaviour and body language*</u>

Your body language will give a lot of information to your prospective employer. Did you know that between 60-90% of the impression you make on others is informed by body language? Your interviewer will be subconsciously affected by this throughout the interview. Use this to your advantage by being aware of the signals you are sending.

- Keep your shoulders back and relaxed in an open, non-threatening pose.

- Plant both feet on the ground to keep yourself stable and grounded.
- Put your hands on the table. People who place their hands under the table can come across as having something to hide.
- If there is a table, make sure you're not too close to it. As a rule of thumb, if your elbows are on the table, move back.
- No table? Rest your hands in your lap.

Other important reminders include: turn off your mobile phone, be polite and courteous, and aim to be confident in your abilities without being arrogant.

Casual

Remember that an interview is always a formal situation. You may become more relaxed throughout the interview, but don't let yourself fall into casual behaviour. Endeavour to remain professional and focused throughout.

Dress

Please dress appropriately. That means absolutely no denim, leather, or flip-flops. If you want to be taken seriously, you'll need to dress in professional attire. For men, this means a plain top, shirt, or polo shirt with shorts. For women, a polo shirt or a blouse with shorts, skirt, skort, or even a dress. Remember to keep whatever you're wearing plain. That means no patterns, prints, or logos. Finally, don't forget your feet. Smart shoes are a must. Ballet pumps or deck shoes are appropriate.

Enthusiasm

Remember to be enthusiastic throughout the interview. Reinforce that you want to work for them and that you believe you're the right person for the job.

Fidgeting

As the saying goes: "You never get a second chance to make a first impression".

It only takes a matter of seconds for a person to make a snap judgment, but this impression is likely to last. Do your best to make a good one by sitting calmly and still. Do your absolute best not to fidget.

Gaze

Keep eye contact with the interviewer throughout, but don't stare. If there's more than one person interviewing you, look at the others on the panel to ensure everyone is engaged and involved.

Handshake

It may be old-fashioned, but a good handshake still goes a long way towards helping you make a strong first impression! Always offer a firm handshake, but make sure you don't crush their hand. Avoid limp handshakes. You are trying to create a statement that you are assertive.

Integrity

Answer *all* questions honestly. Remember, this is yachting. If you get the job, your employers and colleagues will also be your housemates. Anything you say that isn't true will almost certainly come to light.

Jewellery

Simplicity is key, so keep jewellery and piercings to a minimum. Men should stick to a watch and a wedding ring if married.

Knowledgeable

Research the job role and the industry in advance to show you are knowledgeable and prepared.

Listen

Though you may be nervous, try not to talk over the interviewer. Listen carefully to what is being said and asked of you, and take your time formulating answers.

Motivation

It's important for crew members to have plenty of motivation. Show that you're suitable for the job by reflecting on a time or situation when you had to motivate yourself.

Nerves

Nerves affect almost all of us, and your interviewer will make allowances for this. Try to concentrate on what is being said and enjoy the experience. No matter what happens, this interview will be a learning curve that will make you a better candidate. Breathe deeply and slowly to try to keep calm. Remember that we're all human and that no one will judge you for being nervous!

Optimistic

Even if your interviewer tells you there are several other candidates being considered for the position, remain optimistic. They have taken the time to meet with you, which means you are also very much in the running.

Yachting is a time-pressured industry, and no one will be interviewing you just to be polite.

Positive

Keep your answers upbeat and positive. This is important, as no one wants to recruit a negative person.

Questions

Be ready to answer questions such as:
- Why are you interested in this particular role?
- What are your weaknesses? It's okay to highlight them. None of us are perfect, but do try to put a positive spin on them.
- Why do you want to work on this boat, or what is it about this position that interests you?
- What are your short-term goals?
- What are your long-term goals? Employers will be looking for someone who is driven and wants a long career in the yachting industry
- What positive things would your last employer say about you?

To show your interest and intelligence, you should also ask questions in return about:
- The yacht
- Your duties
- Crew dynamics

- The itinerary
- The owners or repeat guests, obviously without asking them to divulge sensitive information
- The level of service expected

References

Before every interview, make sure your reference details are up-to-date and that email addresses and phone numbers are correct. Also, take along a printed copy of any written references you have.

Smile

Smiling will make you appear approachable and friendly. It will also make you feel better, especially if you're really nervous.

Tips and benefits

While it may be tempting to ask about salary, bonuses, and tips, remember that the yachting industry is full of 'fly by nights' who are looking to make quick money. You can make sure you don't get put in this category by waiting for the interviewer to explain the package and benefits on offer in their own time, which they should do!

Um, uh

Try to eliminate verbal fillers such as "uh" and "um." Enlist a friend to ask you sample questions and record the results. When you listen back, pay particular attention to your verbal presentation.

Voice

Enunciate your words. Take a deep breath before answering each question and speak slowly. This will help to stop you tripping over words and may also prevent rambling.

Walk

When you walk in and out of your interview, stand tall with your head up high and shoulders back. No slouching, please

X-Factor

Here's a question. Do you think you have the X-Factor? What is the one thing you have to offer than other candidates don't? Think about what they are looking for and whether you meet the criteria for the perfect candidate in advance.

You

The interview is your opportunity to really sell yourself as a potential crew member. Be eager to highlight your accomplishments and explain your qualifications thoroughly. Prepare yourself for this by re-reading your CV.

Zest

In an industry where there are multiple qualified candidates for every position, it becomes even more important to show your passion and interest for the industry. Let the zest in your personality shine through.

What to do after the interview

- Before you say goodbye, give positive feedback on the interview, thank them for their time, and ask when you're likely to hear back about the position.

- If you have another interview or job offer to consider, let them know. This may affect the speed at which they give you an answer.

- It's good manners to send a follow-up email after the interview to thank the interviewer for their time. Use this opportunity to re-confirm your interest in the position. If you do not have their direct contact details, then you can email the agent who put you up for the position, as they will be sure to pass the message on.

- Do not ask if there's a position for your boyfriend or girlfriend, or give any indication that you would leave at the first sign of a job with your partner.

- Do not assume that the interview is over just because you've left the room. The interviewer may see you make your way out of the building or port, so don't light up a cigarette or make a phone call while you're still in view.

- Don't forget that an interview is a two-way proposition. It's an opportunity for you to find out about the work that will be expected of you and if the boat and the environment are a good fit. Take some time after the interview to consider whether you would want to accept the position if it were offered.

Top tips for Skype interviews

Skype interviews have become relatively common in the yachting industry. While they haven't replaced face-to-face interviews, a Skype interview can be a possibility if you are not based near the yacht when you apply for a position. This type of virtual interview allows potential employers to get a general feeling about you in order to decide whether they want to ask you to travel for a full interview or trial.

Though a Skype interview may feel less formal than a face-to-face interview, it really isn't. You still need to prepare thoroughly.

Before the Interview

- **Username** - Ensure you have a sensible Skype username. Try to use your real name. Something colourful will not give the right impression.

- **Profile picture** – Choose an appropriate photo along the same lines as the one used on your CV. This is important, as your interviewers will see your profile picture. If you have an audio-only interview, then it'll be what they're looking at for the duration of the call.

- **Internet** – Make sure you have a good Internet connection. Do a couple of tests well in advance, and if necessary, make arrangements to use the Internet elsewhere for your call.

- **Sound** – Check to make sure that the audio is working ahead of time.

- **Surroundings** – Position your laptop with a neutral wall behind you and make sure your surroundings look tidy and organised. If you have housemates, make sure they know you are not to be disturbed.

- **Background noise** – Make sure there's no background noise such as music, appliances or nearby conversations. You should also turn off your phone and close down any other programs on your laptop that may sound notifications. It will be very off-putting if the interviewer can hear Facebook notifications in the background. They will likely feel that you're not 100% engaged in the conversation.

- **Documents** – Have a copy of your CV in front of you and prepare a link to your CV, training certificates, and references ready to send in case the interviewer asks for them during the call.

- **Appearance** – You may only be meeting virtually, but the same rules for appearance and clothing apply as if you were attending a face-to-face interview. This advice stands regardless of the time difference.
- **Questions** – Try and keep the interviewer engaged by having interesting questions prepared for them.
- **Practice** – Have a practice Skype interview with a friend. Ask them what your surroundings look like, how clear you are, if they are having any trouble hearing you, and if you look smart enough.

During the interview

Try to look at the camera, not at the screen. It's very tempting to watch yourself or your interviewer during a Skype session, but looking directly at the video camera will enable you to maintain direct eye contact.

Just like in a face-to-face meeting, you need to be aware of your body language. Not all physical cues translate from in-person interviews to Skype interviews, so the ones that do are even more important. Be sure to have good posture, relax your shoulders, and smile. Try not to fidget too much as this can be distracting for the interviewer!

Speak clearly and slowly to ensure your interviewer can hear you. If you miss anything they say due to the connection, ask them politely to repeat it.

After the interview

Once the interview is over, send a follow-up email later that day or the next morning. Do not send a message on Skype, as this is too intrusive and overly familiar. Thank them for their time and express that you are still interested in the position.

Bonus interview tip: use high emotional awareness

If you really want to make a good impression at an interview (and when meeting people in general), aim to follow the principles of Emotional Awareness. This is a technique that empowers you to identify both your emotions and the emotions of others.

An individual who has practised these skills will be able to remain focused and stay connected with themselves and others in any situation, even stressful ones. Emotional awareness is a primary emotional intelligence skill that can be learned. This can be a great use of your time. Being able to connect to your emotions and have moment-to-moment awareness of how they are influencing your thoughts and actions is the key to understanding yourself and others.

Why is all this important for interviews? Because it's not always the person with the best skills for the job that wins in the end; the successful candidate is more often than not the one with the best people skills. Engaging with people draws them to you and enables you to develop strong mutually beneficial relationships.

Harry's Seafarer Story

Harry is a captain/first officer who holds a Master 3000gt ticket. He is British, 35 years old, and came into the yachting industry after working on Ro-Ro ferries.

Before I got my first yachting position I was working in the North Sea as a 2nd Officer within a company that ran offshore support vessels. I was actually working on their only Ro-Ro ferry, which ran between Aberdeen and Lerwick. It mainly transported lorries full of salmon between the Shetlands and the mainland and may as well have been a fishing boat, as it certainly smelt like one!

A good friend of mine told me about yachting, and it sounded almost too good to be true. I was tired of working with grumpy old men and smelling of fish. Yachting sounded well worth a shot.

Luckily it paid off, and I am now a captain/first officer and absolutely love my job.

Most mornings I am up at 0530 to shower, shave, and be out on deck to get the team ready to start at 0600. There will have been a two-man night team on overnight detailing and starting the setup at first light. Once they turn in to sleep, the day team will need to detail the main guest areas of the deck.

By 0700, we'll need to get the tenders in, and if on anchor, get the platforms ready for any fishing or diving trips. After this, we'll continue general detailing and setting up which normally takes till around 1030. Of course, we also need to be ready for guest requests at all times.

From around 1030 onwards, things start to get busy. Guests usually finish their breakfast around this time, and from here on in, it becomes impossible to timetable a day as things can change in an instant (and normally do!)

There will be numerous things to co-ordinate including fishing and diving trips, helicopter departures and arrivals, relocating to a new position or anchorage, tender runs for shopping or cruising, runs ashore for lunch and dinner, Jet Skis, wakeboarding and water skiing trips, use of all the other water sports equipment, coordinating crew changeovers, and fetching stores and provisions for the chefs. Most days include all of this and more, with a selection of guest requests thrown in for good measure.

As captain/first officer, things will normally quiet down for me around 2200. My last task of the day is always to put together a list of night orders for the late shift (usually things such as washing tenders and the like) so that we're all ready to go again in the morning.

Mary's Seafarer Story

Mary is an Australian 2nd Stewardess, aged twenty-five. She has been in the yachting industry for four years.

I had been living in the UK, but my visa had expired. I was twenty years old and having the time of my life, and I didn't want to go home. A friend of mine was in a similar position, and someone we knew suggested that we try yachting. We loved the idea, and booked one-way tickets to the Cote d'Azur. We stayed in a hostel for the first few nights, then made some friends in Antibes and moved into their shared apartment.

We partied a lot at the Hop Store, which is the local Irish bar. We called this networking, and surprisingly it did actually pay off! One night I met a guy called James, and we got talking and hit it off. Three days later I was on my way back from playing a touch football tournament in Monaco when my new friend James called and said, "You want a job? Come down to the Hop Store." It was 1am already, but I got down there ASAP (via a shower of course) and met a wonderful man who went on to be my first and very favourite captain to date!

I was on my way to the boat in Imperia, Italy at 8am the next day.

I'm pleased to say that people in the industry were always very friendly to me, even when I was just starting out. Perhaps this is because I am very approachable and am always keen to make new friends. There must be something to this as I never dock walked and didn't even sign up with any agencies until my second year in the industry.

Once I got on to my first yacht, I was lucky to find myself with a great crew. They were really helpful and interested in showing me how things were done. Of course, there were a few things that came as a bit of a surprise, like the precision that the interior team were expected to detail the cabins and more. I'll never forget the time I was asked to clean a vacuum cleaner with a Q-tip! Though this was quite an adjustment at first, I now secretly love it.

What else can I say about yachting? It offers a lifestyle that not that many people even know about. It is a fantastic, addictive job with many, great benefits.

Glossary

MCA = Maritime & Coastguard Agency

Who are they: The Maritime and Coastguard Agency (MCA) is a UK executive agency working to prevent the loss of lives at sea. They are responsible for implementing both British and international maritime law and safety regulations.

What do they do? The MCA does everything and anything to ensure safe operation of vessels at sea. This includes providing legislation and guidance on maritime matters as well as awarding certification to eligible seafarers.

RYA = Royal Yachting Association

Who are they: The RYA is a national governing body for boating training. The qualifications they award are recognised all over the world.

What do they do? The RYA issues training standards and certification for all forms of boating, including dinghy and yacht racing, motor and sail cruising, RIBs and sports boats, powerboat racing, windsurfing, inland cruising, narrowboats, and personal watercraft.

PYA = Professional Yachting Association

Who are they? The PYA is a not-for-profit association run for crew by crew.

What do they do? Currently, PYA is the only professional body in the world that can verify sea service on yachts for both the Maritime and Coastguard Agency (MCA), and Transport Malta (TM).

You can apply for a PYA Service book, which is part of the PYA membership package. As part of the application process, all your certificates and sea service testimonials will be sighted, verified and stamped. This procedure is accepted by the MCA and means you won't have to send testimonials to the MCA when applying for or revalidating a certificate of competency.

MLC 2006 = The Maritime Labour Convention

What is MLC? The MLC provides protection at work for the world's seafarers.

What do they do? The convention is comprehensive and sets out in one document every seafarer's right to decent working conditions. It covers almost every aspect of their work and onboard life including:
- Minimum age
- Employment agreements
- Hours of work and rest
- Payment of wages

- Paid annual leave
- Repatriation at the end of contract
- Onboard medical care
- The use of licensed private recruitment and placement services
- Accommodation, food and catering
- Health and safety protection and accident prevention
- Seafarers' complaint handling

You can read more about the MLC by visiting the following website: http://www.ilo.org/global/standards/maritime-labour-convention/what-it-does/WCMS_219665/lang--en/index.htm

What does CoC & CeC stand for?

CoC stands for Certificate of Competency / CeC stands for Certificate of Equivalency

What does NOE stand for?

NOE stands for Notice of Eligibility. If you work in the deck team, you will need to send off a Notice of Eligibility (NOE) form to the MCA, along with your training record book in order to complete MCA assessments.

When you've acquired enough sea service to sit an oral examination with the MCA, you will be required to apply for an NOE. This form can be downloaded from the MCA website:

https://www.gov.uk/government/publications/mgn-69-oral-examination-syllabi. All forms must be submitted along with the required supporting documentation.

Please note the MCA takes between four to six weeks to process your NOE and note you cannot book your oral exam until you are in possession of your NOE.

If you are successful in your oral exam, your NOE will then be stamped and signed by the examiner.

What does LIA stand for?

LIA stands for Letter of Initial Assessment. The LIA is for yacht engineer candidates with previous relevant experience or previous sea service. It is the documentation you send to the MCA if you are just entering the yachting industry and want any transferable experience or sea service to be taken into account.

You can apply to the MCA for a Letter of Initial Assessment, which will tell you what level you can enter the industry at and the suggested career route to take. The MCA will require details of any qualifying sea service, engineering qualifications and any apprenticeship served, together with your STCW and medical certificates.

You can download an application from the MCA website:

https://www.gov.uk/government/uploads/system/uploads/attachment data/file/330599/LIA_App_Form_All_Rev_0713.pdf.

It will generally take around four to six weeks to receive a response.

Thank you

This book with written with the new seafarer in mind to give them as much advice and support as possible. My journey in the yachting industry really happened by chance. The majority of it has been on land. I have met some of the most incredible and influential people who have made a huge impact on both my career and personal life.

I believe if you are given the right guidance then you can succeed at whatever it is your heart desires, but sometimes we need someone to guide us and help us find our way.

This book would not be possible without the loving support of my nearest and dearest. He has over two decades experience in the maritime industry, so he not only has given me his support but also provided lots of hands-on knowledge and information passed onto you in this book. There are also the real-life crew stories, so a huge thank you to Daisy, David, Victoria, Simon, Gemma, Heather, Olivia, Chiara, Emily, Alistair, and Graham.

I'd love you to stay in touch with me and let me know how you are doing on your journey. Also, if you need any help or handy hints, I'm here. I am also open to adding any information you feel is missing from this book. You can email me at **hello@career-concierge.com** if its recruitment related then please introduce yourself clare@yotspot.com

The Career Concierge offers

- CV Writing
- Recruitment in conjunction with Yotspot, make sure to register online www.Yotspot.com
- Coaching/Mentoring

Check out our website: www.career-concierge.com

Connect with us on social media

Pintrest: https://uk.pinterest.com/CareerConcierg/
Twitter: https://twitter.com/CareerConcierg
Instagram: https://www.instagram.com/career_concierge/
Facebook: **https://www.facebook.com/careerconcierge.superyachtcv/**
Facebook Group:
https://www.facebook.com/careerconcierge.superyachtcv/
LinkedIn: https://www.linkedin.com/company/careerconcierge

If you have the courage to begin, then you have the courage to succeed

Resources

http://seascopemaritimetraining.com/

www.mcga.gove.uk

http://www.mntb.org.uk/

www.zephyr-yachting.com

http://www.ilo.org/global/lang--en/index.htm

http://www.mlc2006.com/

http://www.rya.org.uk/

http://www.warsashsuperyachtacademy.com/home.aspx

http://www.timeout.com/barcelona/travel/public-transport

http://en.wikipedia.org/

Copyright and Disclaimer

All rights reserved no part of this publication may be reproduced, stored or transmitted in any form or by any means without prior written permission, nor be otherwise circulated in any form of binding or cover other than that in which it is published.

While we have done our best to ensure that all information is correct, we cannot be held responsible for any errors, changes or amendments made since the publication of this book in 2016.

Written and arranged by Clare Dowding, with contributions from seafaring crew and colleagues.

Cover photo by Tim Davison

Copy Editing: Katie M Anderson

Arrangement: Phil Towle

Graphics: Gordon Lundie

Editor: Marjorie Kramer

Copyright © Superyacht Cv Company 2016 / Career Concierge 2017

Printed in Great Britain
by Amazon